D £3.00

THE CROSS IN THE
OLD TESTAMENT

H. Wheeler Robinson

THE CROSS IN THE
OLD TESTAMENT

SCM PRESS LTD
BLOOMSBURY STREET LONDON

First impression 1955
Second impression 1956
Third impression 1960
Fourth impression 1965

PRINTED IN GREAT BRITAIN BY OFFSET LITHOGRAPHY BY
BILLING AND SONS LTD., GUILDFORD AND LONDON

PUBLISHER'S NOTE

IN response to many and repeated requests for the re-publication of Dr. H. Wheeler Robinson's three monographs, originally printed under the titles *The Cross of Job* (1916), *The Cross of the Servant* (1926), and *The Cross of Jeremiah* (1925), we are now offering the three works in a composite volume in the hope that they will be of renewed service. With the exception of *The Cross of Job*, of which the second revised edition (Religion and Life Books, March 1938) is to be found in this volume, no change has been made to the original text. Appendices and bibliographies which are now dated have, however, been omitted.

CONTENTS

I

THE CROSS OF JOB

PREFACE TO THE SECOND EDITION

THE first edition of this little book, published in 1916 (the date is significant), has been out of print for some years. I am led to believe, by repeated requests for its re-publication, that it has still a service to render. There is not much that has called for alteration. I am still as convinced as ever that the author of the Book of Job *does* intend to make a contribution to the problem of innocent suffering, and that the contribution is to be found not simply in the divine utterances that teach the lesson of humility, but also in the suggestion of the prologue, that such suffering may unconsciously serve the divine purpose. Emphasis on this point is the distinctive feature in this exposition of the Book.

H. WHEELER ROBINSON

Oxford
   Christmas Eve 1937

SYNOPSIS

INTRODUCTION

Essential features of all great literature: a subject of permanent interest and a living relation to its age; this exemplified in the Book of Job.

Date and character of the Book; its form and literary structure.

1. Prologue in prose (i and ii).

2. The Debate in poetry (iii-xxxi).
   (*a*) iv-xiv; (*b*) xv-xxi; (*c*) xxi-xxxi.

3. The (later) Elihu speeches in poetry (xxxii-xxxvii).

4. The storm-speeches of Yahweh in poetry (xxxviii-xlii, 6).

5. Epilogue in prose (xlii, 7-17).

Method of study.

I. THE PROBLEM AS VIEWED BY JOB

The change from prosperity to adversity.

Emergence of the problem through the attitude of the friends:

Why do the innocent suffer?

The development of self-revelation, and the final attitude.

(Contrast the defiance of Prometheus, the fatalism of the Mohammedan and the renunciation of the Buddhist.)

II. THE PROBLEM AS VIEWED BY HIS FRIENDS

Varieties of one type: moral retribution in divine government. Job a sinner because a sufferer.

Eliphaz the Mystic.

Bildad the Traditionalist.

Zophar the Dogmatist.

(The later Elihu emphasizes suffering as chastening.)

Inadequacy of this doctrine of retribution to explain innocent suffering.

III. THE PROBLEM AS CREATED AND HANDLED BY YAHWEH[1]

Epilogue: 'double for all his shame'.

The storm-speeches; the wisdom and power of God in nature.

Prologue: the divine purpose. hidden from Job.

IV. THE PROBLEM IN RELATION TO THE CHRISTIAN FAITH

The later belief in immortality.

The Cross of Christ and His insistence on cross-bearing.

Job and the Servant of Yahweh in relation to Christ.

Cosmic Atonement and 'complementary' cross-bearing.

The solidarity of the race.

The permanent value of the Book of Job.

[1] 'Yahweh' is used throughout this book as the correct transliteration of the Hebrew name for God, wrongly spelt as 'Jehovah', and usually translated in the Bible, 'the LORD'.

(Useful modern translations are those by J. E. McFadyen, in *The Wisdom Books in Modern Speech*, and by J. M. Powis Smith, in *The Bible: an American Translation* (1935).)

CONTENTS

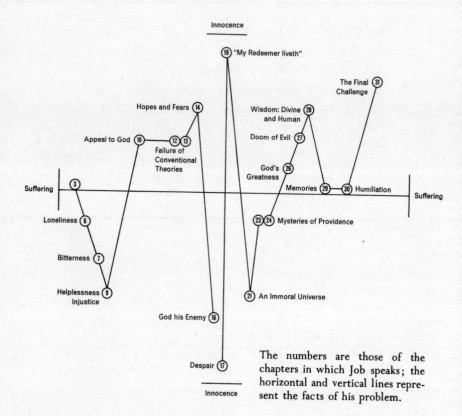

The numbers are those of the chapters in which Job speaks; the horizontal and vertical lines represent the facts of his problem.

INTRODUCTION

ALL great literature has two essential features. It must deal
with some subject of permanent interest, the concern of no
single generation but of all the ages; it must touch the great
things of our common humanity, which the changing years
cannot touch. On the other hand, great literature is always
more or less closely related to the particular age of its production; it comes to its permanent subject through the transient
conditions of that age, and makes them the text of its sermon,
or rather, the mould or pattern into which its raw material
is shaped. The men who have taught us most have never
divorced themselves from the life of their own time; but they
lived and thought so intensely in that time that they have
penetrated through it into the realm of eternal truths. Virgil
wrote the *Æneid* because he felt the majesty and dignity of
Roman destinies; his work has long outlived the Empire it
celebrated. Dante was an ardent politician in the thirteenth-
century strife of Pope and Emperor, city and city; he has compelled the men of all generations to study the insignificant
events of his age in order to understand his vision of unseen
things. Milton incorporated the ideas of Protestant theology,
as Dante did of Catholic; yet their poems are much more than
theological pamphlets. It is not otherwise with the Book of
Job, the noblest production of Hebrew poetry. To understand
it marks an epoch in a man's life; but two conditions are
necessary for its understanding. Since it deals with one of
the enduring mysteries of human life, the unexplained presence of suffering in the world, it has no message for us until
we have come to feel something of the pressure and burden
of that mystery, in our own or other lives. But since it is
in form a Semitic poem, written in an environment so different
from that of modern Western civilization, it can be understood only by patient study of that environment, and, above

15

all, only by putting aside the preconceptions with which many people approach the Bible, preconceptions which rob God of the liberty of speaking to us in His own way.

We do not know who wrote the Book of Job; no information on this point is given us either in the book itself or elsewhere, in any reliable tradition. The central figure of the Book of Job is named twice elsewhere in the Bible; by Ezekiel (xiv. 14, 20) as a type of righteousness, and by James (v. 11) as a type of endurance. Job appears in Mohammedan legend; he swears to give his wife a hundred stripes when he gets well, but Allah tells him to let her off with one blow from a hundred-leaved palm branch. We cannot tell when Job lived. The scene of the Book of Job is laid in Arabia in the remote patriarchal period. It is probable that the actual Job was a man of great possessions and piety, who suffered unexampled misfortunes, his name being handed from one generation to another until it became proverbial. It is of much more interest to us that somewhere between 500 and 400 B.C., that is, within the fifth century before Christ, an unknown author appropriated the tradition, just as Shakespeare did that of King Lear. But he did not simply use it like Shakespeare to draw a picture of human life in its sorrows and afflictions; this unknown Hebrew writer was not only an artist but also a moralist and theologian, with an explicit philosophy of life to declare. He wanted to protest against the current doctrine that suffering and sin always went together; he wanted to prove that there is a mystery in suffering which cannot be wholly understood by man, a mystery that goes back to God, and results in the fact that the innocent can suffer as well as the guilty. His work was probably done not long after the time of that other unknown writer we call Deutero-Isaiah (Isa. xl-lv). Both writers, who have many points of contact, are impressed by the misfortunes of Israel in exile, and especially by the suffering of the innocent in the common lot of the nation. But whereas Deutero-Isaiah has centred his thoughts on the figure of the Suffering Servant of Yahweh, the personified Israel who accomplishes Yahweh's work through his sorrows,[1] the author of Job has addressed himself rather to the general problem

[1] See 'The Cross of the Servant', p. 65 *passim*.

of innocent suffering, which was coming more and more to engage the attention of thoughtful Israelites. He has dealt with this problem in characteristic Hebrew fashion by taking the concrete traditional figure of Job, and by throwing back his own thoughts into the remote age in which Job was supposed to have lived. We must not, then, mistake the general antiquity of the picture of Job in the book for evidence of a date equally remote; as a matter of fact it would have been as inconceivable a product of Israel's life in that remote age as would be Tennyson's *In Memoriam* in the times of the early Britons. In both cases, the problems discussed arise only in a comparatively late stage of civilization.

The Book of Job itself distinguishes between the traditional story of Job and the discussion of the problem of innocent suffering by putting the former in prose and the latter in verse. The Revised Version shows that the Prologue to the Book (cc. i and ii) is in prose, as is also the Epilogue (xlii. 7-17). It is possible that this prose story was already in existence and was appropriated or adapted by the author of the poetry, but, in any case, it is integral to his purpose. The rest of the Book, apart from merely connecting links, is in Hebrew poetry. The chief characteristic of Hebrew poetry is what is called ' parallelism '; for example :

> ' There the wicked cease from troubling
> And there the weary are at rest.'

There is no rhyme, as there is in much modern poetry, nor any exact counting of syllables or attention to the quantity or length of the syllables; but there is a loose rhythm, which has its own impressiveness. All through the poem we shall note the Semitic love of the concrete; the argument prefers pictures to abstract statements. The poem is dramatic, without being a drama in the full sense of the word. The debate between Job and his friends goes on in three cycles (cc. iii-xxxi); it is followed by a series of speeches by a certain Elihu, which most scholars regard as a later addition to the book (xxxii-xxxvii), and by the speeches of Yahweh out of the storm (xxxviii-xlii, 6).

B

The action of this dramatic poem is internal, not external; it centres in the development of Job's own thought in presence of his problem. This suggests the most effective method of studying the book as a whole. We shall try to do what Browning did in *The Ring and the Book*. He told us the same story a dozen times over, putting it from different standpoints, and leaving us to draw our own conclusions. The author of the Book of Job has given us a number of different attitudes to the problem of suffering; he, too, has partly left us to draw our own conclusions. We shall therefore begin with the central figure, and, at some length, try to understand the gradual unfolding of his thought. We shall then see how the same problem presents itself to the friends who discuss it with him. Further, the Book shows us an altogether different standpoint, that of Yahweh Himself; in this we must suppose that the author's chief message to us will lie. Finally, we shall see what further light is thrown upon the problem by our Christian faith. It may seem strange that we do not begin with the Prologue, if this is to be regarded as containing the author's ultimate explanation of Job's sufferings. But it should be remembered that the scene of this explanation is laid in heaven; it is hidden from all those who take part in the dialogue. To understand what *they* say and think, we must try to stand where they do. We shall therefore endeavour in the first place to trace the words and thought of the central person, knowing no more than he is supposed to know.

I

THE PROBLEM AS VIEWED
BY JOB

WE are to listen, then, to a single voice, telling out in naked
self-revelation the story of a spiritual agony. A man suffering the torment of physical and mental pain does not think
logically and progressively. His thoughts are instinctive.
They fly out like sparks struck from the iron as it lies between
the hammer of God and the anvil of life. At one moment
they are bright and fierce, at another dim and dull. We are
to mark 'the incidents in the development of a soul', of which
a great writer once said, 'little else is worth study'. We shall
note the various changes of mood, and find the throbs of
anguish becoming the birth-pangs of truth. We shall indeed
hear the sound heard in the last century by an English poet
and thinker, as he stood on Dover beach—'the melancholy,
long, withdrawing roar' of the sea of faith. But the ebb of
that sea will be followed by the flow; the turn of the tide will
come, and all around the island of this lonely but faithful
soul, the sea of faith will rise again up 'the vast edges drear
and naked shingles of the world'. It is this startling sincerity
of utterance, combined with the nature of the subject, that
makes the Book of Job so modern in its appeal. For we feel
that this is not simply literature. It is life, distilled life. The
utterance can be as fierce and terrible as an awakened volcano,
as broad and swift as one of the great rivers, as full of sombre
peace in its rarer moments of repose as an autumn sunset.

We must begin, however, with the conditions which give
rise to the problem on the rack of which Job is stretched. In
the opening verses of the Book he was introduced to us as
a man unvexed by doubt. So far from his life raising any
problem at all, it was one of the most convincing arguments
to his own age that faith in God was fully warranted. The

conditions under which he lived perfectly satisfied the conventional theories of religion. Spiritual health and material wealth were in exact proportion; in both respects he was 'the greatest of all the children of the East'. A particular example of his piety is given, in order that we may realize its depth. He is careful concerning the lightest sins of ignorance, not only in himself, but also in his family; he regularly intercedes for them with God. It is a man of such exemplary religion who suddenly becomes the protagonist in a tragedy. He has walked the stage of life in simple dignity, but now a fierce glare of limelight beats upon him, to show him reeling under blow upon blow. The hardest blow of all is the unanswered 'Why?' The real problem is created for Job by the fact that *he* did not stand among the sons of God who discussed his fate. The hiding of God's power was the dazzling light of an unknown divine purpose, a purpose which to Job was purposeless. Everyone is familiar with the vividly drawn series of catastrophes which deprives him of all his possessions. They proceed to a climax, the least valuable part of his property being lost first, and his beloved children last; they are balanced and contrasted with great artistic effect. The first and third, the loss of the oxen and of the camels, come through human agency, the second and fourth, the loss of sheep and of children, are due to what we should call natural causes also, the lightning and the desert wind, though the Hebrew conceived these as the direct and supernatural activities of God. The fifth and crowning disaster is the hideous disease of leprosy, which was regarded as a peculiar mark of divine displeasure. Its result is to make him not only the sufferer of intense physical pain, but also an outcast from the civilization of his time. Away from the dwelling-place of men, he lies on the burnt dung-heaps which are a familiar feature of the neighbourhood of Oriental villages; there we must picture him through all the cycles of colloquy, for there his friends find him. Thither comes his wife, with her so natural outburst, womanly in the depth of her sympathy with the sufferer, angry with God because of her love for Job. Blake's fine illustration, as Bradley has pointed out, conceives her to be with him to the very end, the faithful sharer of his sorrows as before of his joys. This has no warrant in the Book, but it has no contradiction. Unlike her sympathy, that of the friends is at first unspoken. It is very real, however much disturbed by the thought that divine retribution must be at work.

It is contact with the silent sympathy of the friends that makes Job break at last his long silence in the outburst of grief that forms the third chapter. Here the real problem is as yet unrealized by Job. We listen simply to pent-up sorrow breaking out in natural language, a groaning and travailing as of the brute creation, unaccentuated by thought on the mystery behind. 'Better never born; better dead at birth; why is death withheld from me now?'[1] The most significant feature here is the picture given of the Under-world (iii. 13-19). For Job and his contemporaries there is practically no thought of life after death. The ghosts of men indeed linger on in Sheol, like the pale and bloodless shades pictured by Homer in Hades; but this is not worth calling life, and counts for nothing in the common thought of men. Good and bad alike go down to its depths when life is over; there they live a sort of dream-life, unless some witch of Endor disturbs them. This dark and gloomy cavern (cf. Isa. xiv. 3 ff., and Ezek. xxxii, 17 ff.) is all that Job can expect after death, though we shall see gleams of a larger hope play fitfully across the uninviting background. The fact is important, because it deepens the problem when once that has arisen. The vindication of Job's righteousness must come on earth, if it is to come at all.

What is it, then, that brings the real problem before Job? It is the declared attitude of his friends to the fact of his suffering. It had never crossed his mind that his agony could be regarded as the punishment for sin. He had, perhaps, never doubted the conventional theory of retribution, which drew an exact balance of desert and fortune on this side of the grave. But when he realizes that his friends are applying the theory to himself, he starts back with horror, as from the brink of some darkness-hidden cliff, whose yawning depth a flash of lightning has revealed. They are saying to him that which Nathan said to David: 'Thou art the man.' But there

[1] iii. 3-10, is modelled on Jer. xx. 14-18.

is this difference; whereas David suddenly saw himself as others saw him, Job realized that the orthodox doctrine of his age was false, false at least as to himself. He knew in his heart that he was innocent of any sin great enough to explain the magnitude of his sufferings. But if the theory would not fit his own case, how could he go on applying it to others? His creed was destroyed; but the living faith within him persisted in putting forth new shoots. 'I am innocent; I do not know why God has sent all this trouble upon me. It looks as if there were no justice, no right or wrong in life at all; and yet, and yet—God *must* somehow right the wrong. It can't be true that I have heard His last word.'

It agrees with the way in which the problem rises that the dominant note of the sixth chapter should be that of loneliness. In a graphic Oriental figure, Job makes us see what he had looked for, what he expected to find in the silent sympathy of his friends. He describes a company of travellers through the waterless desert, whose water-skins have failed them. Let an Eastern traveller's words (Richard Burton's) make the figure living to us:

'Above, through a sky terrible in its stainless beauty, and the splendours of a pitiless, blinding glare, the Samun caresses you like a lion with flaming breath. Around lie drifted sand-heaps, upon which each puff of wind leaves its trace in solid waves, flayed rocks, the very skeletons of mountains, and hard unbroken plains, over which he who rides is spurred by the idea that the bursting of a water-skin, or the pricking of a camel's foot, would be a certain death of torture—a haggard land infested with wild beasts and wilder men—a region whose very fountains murmur the warning words, "Drink and away!"'

'I turned to you,' Job says, 'as despairing travellers turn to some remembered wady, some valley in which a plentiful stream supplied refreshment in other days. I turned to you—and lo! my wady was dried up with the drought of summer heat.' 'To him that is ready to faint kindness should be showed from his friend, even to him that forsaketh the fear of the Almighty.'

The natural sequence of the loneliness of chapter vi is the bitterness of chapter vii—bitterness against God who is responsible for all this pain, and sorrow. We note the significant difference here from a frequent modern attitude. The instinct of a *modern* Job would be to doubt the very existence of God, and to think himself the sport of cruel circumstance, the mere plaything of natural law. Such an attitude is possible to the doubter of to-day, because science has opened up to us a great world of Nature, which seems to be able to go on by itself, at least to the superficial thinker. But Hebrew thought could not so easily dispense with a very present God, whether or no He was a help in trouble. It had to think of God in order to account for the world; it had not learnt to make the secondary causes of Nature primary, and to deify Nature herself. Thus it is that through all Job's thinking the reality of God's *existence* remains unchallenged. The whole controversy is fought around His alleged *character*. Is God at heart good or bad? The bitter resentment of Job is expressed in a striking way. After speaking of God's relentless pursuit of him, even in his dreams, he passes to a startling parody of the eighth Psalm, which turns its faith into doubt, and its gratitude into revolt:

'What is man, that thou shouldest magnify him,
And that thou shouldest set thine heart upon him,
And that thou shouldest visit him every morning,
And try him every moment?' (vii. 17, 18).

This bitter mood passes in the ninth chapter into more explicit statement of his own helplessness against the divine injustice. 'I admit the power of God,' Job says, 'but what is the use of God's power to me, when it is used against me?' Job can say, 'From the first, Power was—I knew'; but his agony is too great for him yet to say:

'Life has made clear to me,
That, strive but for closer view,
Love were as plain to see.'

God is unjust; man, even when innocent, is helpless and

hopeless before a God who conforms to no standard of right in the exercise of His power. Is life, then, worth living?

> ' I despise my life;
> It is all one; therefore I say,
> He destroyeth the perfect and the wicked.
> If the scourge slay suddenly,
> He will mock at the trial of the innocent' (ix. 21-23).

Think what that terrible phrase means—the jeering God. The Hebrew word suggests the stammering, chuckling derision of brutal and half-idiotic mirth. God has become to Job a sort of Gulliver, straddling over Lilliput. Quite in the spirit of such a figure is the reference to the dirty ditch (ix. 30):

> ' If I wash myself with snow,
> And make my hands never so clean,
> Yet wilt thou plunge me in the ditch.
> And mine own clothes shall abhor me.'

No man can hold long to such a belief about God, whilst retaining his sanity. By one of those revulsions of feeling which characterize such a history as this, Job returns to a better spirit, in which we can mark the chastened note of appeal to God. He forgets the wild outbreak of his imagination, and is touched into a moment's hope by a characteristic Hebrew thought—the infinite pains God has taken in weaving together the human body of the unborn child (x. 8, 9):

> ' Thine hands have framed me and fashioned me
> Together round about; yet thou dost destroy me.
> Remember, I beseech thee, that thou hast fashioned me
> as clay :
> And wilt thou bring me into dust again? '

Perhaps Tennyson had those words in his mind when he wrote :

'Thou madest Life in man and brute;
Thou madest Death; and lo, thy foot
Is on the skull which thou hast made.

'Thou wilt not leave us in the dust:
Thou madest man, he knows not why,
He thinks he was not made to die;
And thou hast made him: thou art just.'

Job's appeal to God's creative purpose really contradicts his late outburst; he is not himself convinced of the charges of injustice which he brings against God. But through all this part of the poem we are moving in the realm of instinctive feeling rather than of reasoned thought. It is to the provocation of the debate that we owe the more intellectual and reasoned treatment of the problem in the twelfth and thirteenth chapters. We need not here consider Job's criticism of those conventional theories of suffering which his friends offer him. Some sentences from the thirteenth chapter set before us the whole situation. 'Your memorable sayings,' says Job to his friends, 'are proverbs of ashes'; you sit over them, like some shivering wretch over a fire already burnt out. 'Your defences are defences of clay'; the ramparts of war you build that look so solid will crumble like dried clay at the first strong hand that is laid upon them. John Locke called such conventional ideas wealth borrowed from others, which is 'like fairy money, [for] though it were gold in the hand from which he received it, [it] will be but leaves and dust when it comes to use.' Leaves and dust—but Job feels that such things are pictures not only of his friends' arguments, but of himself in shattered frame and nerveless spirit:

'Wilt thou harass a driven leaf?
And wilt thou pursue the dry stubble? . . .
Man is like a rotten thing that consumeth,
Like a garment that is moth-eaten.'

Poor, sad humanity, with no prospect of relief! thinks Job as he passes from the thought of his own sorrows to those

of the world, just as Tennyson passed from his personal loss
in Hallam's death to the whole problem of a mourning world.
In the next chapter (xiv) of 'Hopes and Fears', we meet with
the first of those gleams of light against the darkness of the
future, which come but to vanish again. It is not a faith, still
less a creed, but a mere flash of personal desire. 'If God
would only let me go away at once into the dark underworld,
and let me be there for a time till He had forgotten to be
angry!' Job wants to hide away, like a little child, till the
father's fit of temper is over. 'I would wait quite patiently
down there in spite of the darkness and gloom. One day,
God would suddenly remember, and look round, and miss me,
and cry, "Job, Job, where is my child Job?" And then I,
waiting in some corner of that dreary darkness for His lightest
whisper, would joyfully cry, "Here, Lord, here—ready in
Sheol as was thy servant Isaiah in the temple." I would put
my hand in my Father's, not like the prodigal, for I have never
left Him, but like a happy son who sees his father's long
estrangement pass away' (xiv. 13-15):

'Oh that thou wouldst hide me in Sheol,
  That thou wouldest keep me secret, until thy wrath be past,
  That thou wouldest appoint me a set time and remember
    me!
  If a man die, shall he live again?
  All the days of my warfare would I wait,
  Till my release should come.
  Thou shouldest call and I would answer thee:
  Thou wouldest have a desire to the work of thine hands.'

It is disappointing to see that splendid hope die away like
the glory of sunset, to see Job so near the truth, trembling,
as it were, on the very verge of a Christian faith in God and
immortality, and then throwing up his hands in despair (xvi).
But that is life; that is you and I and all generations. The
sudden drop is perhaps due to the harsh and untrue line taken
by Eliphaz in the intervening chapter. The unkindness and
the injustice are too much for Job, and he falls to the depths
—deeper depths even than when he thought of God as watch-

ing with derisive scorn the suffering of an innocent man. He portrays God as his active enemy, in a succession of terrible pictures.

God is a beast of prey:

> ' He hath torn me in his wrath and hated me,
> He hath gnashed upon me with his teeth:
> Mine adversary sharpeneth his eyes upon me' (xvi. 9).

It is like looking into the face of a tiger, with no iron bars between. Or God is a Giant Despair:

> ' I was at ease, and he brake me asunder;
> Yea, he hath taken me by the neck, and dashed me to
> pieces:
> He hath also set me up for his mark.
> His archers compass me round about.
> He cleaveth my reins asunder and doth not spare;
> He poureth out my gall upon the ground.
> He breaketh me with breach upon breach;
> He runneth upon me like a giant' (xvi. 12-14).

Given such a conception of God, with power to work His own angry will upon man, there could be no truer courage than that of Job's cry (18):

> ' O earth, cover not my blood,
> And let my cry have no resting-place.'

It was in this spirit that the Greek hero, Prometheus, chained to the rock, defied the unjust Zeus to do his worst:

> ' O Mother venerable!
> O Æther rolling round
> The common light of all,
> See'st thou what wrongs I bear? '

After such thoughts of God, there can be nothing but the unrelieved despair of chapter xvii:

'My days are past, my purposes are broken off . . .
If I hope, Sheol is mine house;
I have spread my couch in the darkness;
I have said to corruption, Thou art my father;
To the worm, Thou art my mother and my sister;
Where then is my hope?
And as for my hope, who shall see it?
It shall go down to the bars of Sheol,
When once there is rest in the dust' (xvii. 11-16).

The famous nineteenth chapter also begins with the pedal notes of despair, deep and solemn with a soul's agony. But it soars aloft, like some Abt Vogler at his organ, into the triumphant chord of anticipated victory—the nearest thing in the Old Testament to Paul's 'Thanks be to God, who giveth us the victory.' That chord is struck in familiar words of sacred associations: 'I know that my Redeemer liveth.' But it does not mean to Job what its use by many a Christian grave has made it mean to us. He has just made one last appeal to his friends for sympathy: 'Have pity on me, have pity on me, O ye my friends, for the Hand of God hath touched me.' The appeal is vain, and for a moment Job dreams of an appeal to posterity:

'Oh that my words were now written!
Oh that they were inscribed in a book!
That with an iron pen and lead
They were graven in the rock for ever!'

But straightway he thinks of a better appeal, an appeal to the same God who seems so cruel. In his heart of hearts he knows that God Himself must some day right the wrong. God will become his 'blood-avenger', for that is what the Hebrew word rendered 'redeemer' really means. In old Semitic law, the next-of-kin received the solemn charge of righting the wrong, and clearing the murdered man's name. So Job's blood will utter its cry to God's ears, and He, of all persons in the universe, He Himself will right the wrong. Job is thus claiming a sort of spiritual kinship with God. God will for His kinsman's sake step down to earth and prove that Job *was* innocent. Job himself will be dead; it will be, he says, 'after my skin has been thus destroyed', that 'without my flesh shall I see God' (25, R.V., mar.). Apparently Job believes that he will be brought up from the underworld as a ghost, like the spirit of Samuel brought up before Saul. Thus will Job see for himself the end of the Lord, that the Lord is very pitiful and of tender mercy. In such confidence Job almost saw the Father, without the Son's manifestation of His glory.

A modern book would probably make the words of Job end on this high note, for the sake of the dramatic effect, if for nothing else. He has found again the God of righteousness and mercy whom he honoured and served in earlier and happier days. We may think it, after all, truer to life that he should take up again his weary argument, and that the words of his friends should bring him down from heaven to earth. This is what happens in the twenty-first chapter, where there is a graphic picture of the wicked man's prosperity. In the twenty-third and twenty-fourth chapters he thinks of God as hiding Himself in the mysteries of Providence. In the twenty-fourth chapter there is a remarkable series of miniature paintings of wickedness. In the twenty-sixth we meet again with the often repeated thought of God's greatness and power (14):

> 'Lo, these are but the outskirts of His ways:
> And how small a whisper do we hear of Him!
> But the thunder of His power who can understand?'

The debate is now concluded, the following chapters (xxvii-xxxi) forming a monologue in several clearly marked portions (though it is probable that the speeches have been wrongly distributed). Chapter xxvii shows a sounder grasp of facts and a saner view of life. Chapter xxviii is probably a later addition to the Book, fully worthy to be added; its point lies in the last verse, which teaches that, whilst God's wisdom is unsearchable, man's is the wisdom of piety and morality. And then Job seems to gather himself together, this time deliberately and of set purpose, for his final challenge of God. He will fling down the gauntlet before God Himself; but first he passes in pathetic review the days of unbroken happiness and respect that were once his, and contrasts with them his present humiliation and suffering.

The noble chapter (xxxi) containing the final challenge of God should be carefully studied by anyone who desires to know what were the ethical ideals of the Hebrews.[2] It is not only a solemn declaration of innocence on the part of Job, but a summary of those duties, social and religious, the performance of which made the 'good man' of that age. It has been rightly said that 'if we want a summary of moral duties from the Old Testament, it might better be found in Job's soliloquy as he turns away from his friends and reviews his past life, than in the Ten Commandments.'

The form of the final challenge employs the metaphor of the law-court (xxxi. 35-37). Job asks for the indictment under which he is being prosecuted and punished. He thinks of God in two capacities at once, that is, as the opponent who is set against him, and as the judge who tries the case. This is an appeal to God against God with the daring illogicality of faith; it is a challenge to the over-God, the real God, to declare the right :

> 'Would that I had a hearer!
> Behold, my mark!
> Let the Almighty answer me!
> Would that I had the document written by my opponent!
> Surely on my shoulder would I carry it,
> I would bind it as a crown unto me;
> The number of my steps would I declare to him,
> Prince-like would I approach him.'

Prince-like—we cannot leave Job with any truer word than that. He has been princely in his despair as well as his hope. He has won the victory of faith over the world, the flesh and the devil. He has refused the suggestion to doubt his own conviction of innocence; he has conquered the temptation to conceive God as ultimately unjust, to which for a time he

---

[2] In form it is an 'oath of purgation' such as an accused man might swear before an earthly tribunal.

yielded. The problem of Job on its theoretical side is as obscure as ever to him; he is quite unable to account for the union of suffering and innocence in his own case, and, as he has come to think, in the case of many others. But he has solved it as a practical problem; he has won through man's theories about God to God himself. Like Hosea, he sees God's love to be deeper than God's wrath. His challenge is really a prayer, and prayer, as a great scholar has rightly said, is the only adequate confession of faith. No place is given to Job, it is true, among the heroes of faith commemorated by the Epistle to the Hebrews; he is too unconventional to fit in very well with any ordered scheme. But we can put him with the man who said, 'Lord, I believe; help thou mine unbelief.' On the face of the brave sufferer the tears of agony are yet undried; but, as the light of God falls on that face, every tear builds its own rainbow of hope, God's mercy-sign. Hidden in the brightness of that light, God weeps Himself; in all our afflictions He is afflicted. But the heart of God is full of joy, because He has not trusted Job in vain with the witness to a disinterested religion and an enduring faith.

There are, as we shall see, other important interpretations of the problem of suffering made by the Book of Job, from the different standpoints which its actors represent. But we may gather together the elements of the contribution made by Job's personal attitude, with the more confidence because the author has made Yahweh explicitly declare to the friends, 'Ye have not spoken of me the thing that is right, as my servant Job hath.' This must mean that, if we put aside Job's passionate words of protest against his fortunes, and think simply of his final attitude, we have at least part of the truth about our problem. Job was justified in holding to his innocence; suffering is no proof of sin. If that has become to us a commonplace, let us learn from such a book as this what it sometimes costs to reach a commonplace, before it has become common. Job was right in appealing to God against the terrible mystery of circumstance. His appeal is an act of faith; it is not defiance; at least, not that in its underlying significance. We have only to compare Job with the somewhat similar figure of Prometheus in Greek poetry to realize this great difference. Prometheus, chained to his rock for bringing divine gifts to men, defies Zeus to do his worst; in that defiance we have the Greek spirit of restless energy, and of boundless confidence in human possibilities. But Job, on his dung-heap, torn not by an eagle, but by leprosy, defies the sufferings which almost overwhelm him to rob him of his faith in a hidden God; in that faith you have the great Hebrew contribution to human history. It may be good to say, heroic to be able to say:

> 'Out of the night that covers me,
>   Black as the pit from pole to pole,
> I thank whatever gods may be
>   For my unconquerable soul.'

But we fling ourselves upon a nobler and greater issue when we can say of God: '*He* is the master of my fate, *He* is the captain of my soul.' Job, as we have seen, does not doubt the divine existence; his bitter struggle relates to the divine character. The victory of his faith here, the conviction that

> 'Nothing can be good in Him,
>   Which evil is in me.'

is essential to any mastery of the problem of suffering that is to be adequate for our Western civilization.

In the great Eastern world there are two attempted solutions of the problem which serve by contrast to illustrate the characteristic contribution of Hebrew thought in the person of Job. Mohammedan fatalism goes back to an imperfect conception of the character of God. Its final answer to the problem of innocent suffering is 'the will of Allah', and the dominant note in the conception of Allah is Power, not Love. Mohammedanism has well been called, in spite of its rigorous monotheism, 'the pantheism of force'. It has inspired, and can inspire, a sublime disregard of the worst suffering; but for us Westerns it is even less possible to accept Allah than the God of Calvin. The very strength of Job's protest shows the difference of his position from the supreme doctrine of Islam—submission. He is a Semite, like the Arab prophet, and the majesty of God is the fundamental thought of the higher Semitic religion. Doughty, who knew the modern Arabs as hardly any other Western, says of them, 'Semites, it is impossible that they should ever blaspheme, in manner of those of our blood, against the Heavenly Providence.' But the great Hebrew prophets of the eighth century had taught Israel to see the majesty of Yahweh not in His power so much as in His moral personality; it is to this that the ultimate appeal of Job lies.

Far removed from Mohammedan fatalism is Buddhist renunciation. Here is a religion, originally without a god, built round the very problem of suffering before us. The message of the Buddha was essentially this : if suffering could not be taken out of life, yet life could be taken out of suffering, by true culture now, and by its fruits hereafter. 'In the midst of sorrow there is no Nirvana, and in Nirvana there is no sorrow.' The Buddhist would have traced Job's present sufferings to his Karma, his moral desert carried over from a previous life. He would have admitted Job's present innocence, and would have preached to him the renunciation of all desire, the surrender of that passionate individuality already unfolded before us. But Job's problem springs from the very assertion of his individuality; this is the datum of his thought. He can no more surrender himself and his conviction of integrity, than he can surrender the character of God; in other words, Buddhist renunciation is as impossible to him as Mohammedan fatalism. In this emphasis on individuality, this conviction of the worth of human life to God, the Christian Gospel is with Job. Rightly has Vinet said of individuality : 'The glory of the Gospel lies in strengthening it in a few, in awakening it in the many, and in purifying it in all.' This uniqueness of human life, this inner experience of living that belongs to each individual and to no one else as to him, has a consequence of profound importance for all religion, and especially for the problem of suffering before us. The great things will have value for us only as they come before us individually; we are not warmed, as Job reminds us, with the ashes of second-hand religion. 'I had heard of thee,' says Job to God, 'with the hearing of the ear, but now mine eye seeth Thee.' That must mean that he has travelled by his own path, the one path that was of any use to him, the path of unflinching sincerity. Thus the Bible has set the stamp of its approval in a marked degree on individual sincerity. Only by sincerity do we reach the intrinsic worth of the values of life, the things really worth having. So men may find at last an inner joy within the suffering that robs it of its worst. Robert Louis Stevenson has reminded us, through the memory of a boys' game with lanterns, that there is a secret and incommunicable element in life, a hidden joy that is *the* life, and that if we miss this we miss all that counts. That is what the friends missed who gazed on Job; they missed the joy at the heart of his sorrow, the joy of his faith in God. 'These things have I spoken unto you, that my joy may be in you.' We shall find, before we have done, that more than one spiritual tie links Job on his dung-heap with Christ in Gethsemane.

II

THE PROBLEM AS VIEWED
BY HIS FRIENDS

So far, we have traced the development of the thought of Job, in presence of the problem: 'How is it possible, in a world morally governed by a just and powerful God, for an innocent man to suffer as I am suffering?' Since he could not resort to the doctrine of human immortality, with its compensations of another life, he was driven at first to the terrible doctrine of divine immorality. Yet his faith in the character of God was victorious, and we left him appealing with confidence to the God he had denounced.

Around this agonized thinker stand his three friends. They have come to him honestly to sympathize with him, but, because they do not understand his trouble, their presence only brings home to him his loneliness. Their well-meant words, uttered in the three rounds of debate into which the central part of the Book is divided, again and again stimulate him to some of his wildest outbreaks. But their arguments are more than part of the machinery of this dramatic poem. They supply the background of conventional religion, which throws him into relief as a daring pioneer, who values truth more than orthodoxy. They are, all three, varieties of one fixed type, the champions of one settled position. The doctrine for which they stand is that of moral retribution as the supreme principle of divine government, though incidentally there are references to the value of suffering in the discipline of character. They are sure that God is righteous and all-powerful; they believe that He is directly concerned with the individual lives of men. It follows that God must punish evil and reward good. So far there is nothing in their argument to which we can object. But they go on to commit a well-known logical fallacy. They say, in effect: All evil-doers are sufferers; Job is a sufferer; therefore Job is an evil-doer.

The fallacy lies in supposing that the class of sufferers is exhausted by the class of evil-doers, and that suffering can spring from no other purpose of God than the will to punish evil. But this is the very heart of the problem of Job—that he has to find a place in his scheme of things for suffering which cannot be penalty and is carried beyond the limits of discipline. Thus, as often happens in debate, *they* never come in sight of the question that racks *his* mind. They go on applying their argument with increasing severity to prove that he must be a sinner because he is a sufferer. But all the time he, knowing that he is innocent of any sin that can call for such suffering, is beating the wings of his spirit like some imprisoned bird against the narrow limits of their faith. He tries to break through the wall of death into a life beyond, of which they do not even dream. He flutters up against the roof of his little world to seek God's purpose, of which they are so sure; they are as dull to the meaning of his appeal as men can be to the song of the lark above their heads.

The three friends belong, as I have said, to one fixed type of thought, the prevailing type in the writer's age, against which he wishes to protest as being utterly inadequate. But, to a certain extent at least, he has differentiated their characters and points of view, and we can give them names which broadly describe these.[1] The foremost of the three is Eliphaz the Mystic. His character as suggested by the three speeches ascribed to him has grace and dignity. He strikes and emphasizes the note of personal experience; he speaks of what he has learnt through many years of fellowship with God. When he has heard Job pray for death, he answers him (iv and v) in gentle and deprecatory words; he recalls the help Job has given to other men in earlier days, and bids Job think

[1] With what follows, it may be of interest to compare the impression made by the three figures on Sir Arthur Quiller-Couch: ' I find Eliphaz more of a personage than the other two; grander in the volume of his mind, securer in wisdom; as I find Zophar rather noticeably a mean-minded grey-beard, and Bildad a man of the stand-no-nonsense kind ' (*On the Art of Reading*, Lect. x).

of his own religious past. Then he declares the truth for which he stands, the doctrine of retribution. 'Who ever perished being innocent, or where were the upright cut off? According as I have seen, they that plough iniquity, and sow mischief, reap the same.' Then follows the most characteristic thing in the speeches of Eliphaz, which justifies the name 'mystic'. In thoughts from the visions of the night he has been caught up into a world of personal experience, which has become the starting-point of his future thought. That which has been brought home to him is the moral majesty of God, and the lowly estate of God's creatures (iv. 12 ff.):

'Now a thing was secretly brought to me,
And mine ear received a whisper thereof.
In thoughts from the visions of the night,
When deep sleep falleth on men,
Fear came upon me and trembling,
Which made all my bones to shake.
Then a breath passed over my face;
The hair of my flesh stood up.
It stood still, but I could not discern the appearance
    thereof,
A form was before mine eyes.
Silence, and I heard a voice:
Can man be righteous before God?
Can man be pure before his Maker?
Behold, He putteth no trust in His servants;
And His angels He chargeth with error.
How much more them that dwell in houses of clay,
Whose foundation is in the dust,
Which are crushed like the moth!'

Eliphaz speaks of this mystical vision, this rare hour which has become the centre of his spiritual life, in order to teach Job the folly of his complaint. How vain it is for man, in all his impurity, to challenge the awful purity of God! Man's only thought in God's presence must be humility; he must think only of God, not of himself, or must think of himself only as utterly dependent on God. Eliphaz warns Job against the

thought that his suffering is purposeless torture, some chance
product of the earth:

> ' Affliction cometh not forth of the dust,
> Neither doth trouble spring out of the ground.'

Think rather, Eliphaz says, that because of your own impurity of nature you are born to trouble; that this is the law
of your life, as natural as it is for the sparks to fly up from
the fire.   He suggests the real cause of Job's sufferings and
the remedy for them:

> ' As for me, I would seek unto God,
> And unto God would I commit my cause.'

He bids Job to despise not the chastening of the Almighty,
and draws a fine picture of Job's latter end—the patriarch
going the round of his folds once more, and once more rejoicing
in his descendants:

> 'Thou shalt come to thy grave in a full age,
> Like as a shock of corn cometh in in its season.'

The real sympathy and affection of this first speech of
Eliphaz ought to remind us that ' Job's comforters ' were not
what they are often represented to be.   They were not cold-
hearted hypocrites; they were good and sincere men, whose
chief defect was that suffering had not unlocked the door for
them into the larger world of Job's thoughts.   It was natural,
if we allow for their standpoint, that their later speeches
should be more severe, as they saw Job hardening himself in
his conviction of innocence.   Thus even Eliphaz, the most
sympathetic of the three, later on strongly resents Job's
criticism of his friends' faith:

> 'Yea, thou doest away with fear,
> And impairest devotion before God ' (xv. 4).

Eliphaz speaks as one of ' the gray-headed and the very aged men, much elder than thy father ', and this, he feels, should entitle him to more respect. Once more Eliphaz returns to his exhortation, the mystic vision of the night:

> ' What is man that he should be clean?
> And he that is born of woman that he should be
> righteous? ' (xv. 14).

If it be objected to his doctrine of absolutely moral retribution that the wicked apparently prosper, Eliphaz has an answer ready, an answer making a real contribution to the argument he presents. He gives a vivid picture of the spiritual sufferings of the conscience-stricken man, in whose ears is a sound of terrors. In every dark corner he sees a sword uplifted, like Macbeth's dagger, to strike him; in his prosperity he must contemplate the time when he will need to beg his bread (xv. 20 ff.). All this has its truth, and makes life other than it often seems (though there is atrophy as well as activity of conscience in the sinner). The closing speech of Eliphaz (xxii) proceeds to draw the last consequence of his doctrine. He directly accuses Job of specific acts of wickedness, since he can account for Job's suffering in no other way. Yet he urges Job to turn in penitence to God, who will then no longer turn from him (26-28):

> ' Then shalt thou delight thyself in the Almighty,
> And shalt lift up thy face unto God.
> Thou shalt make thy prayer unto Him, and He shall hear
> thee . . .
> And light shall shine upon thy ways.'

Much less interest attaches to the figures of Bildad and Zophar than to that of Eliphaz. Bildad can be called the Traditionalist in contrast with the devotional temperament of Eliphaz. He dwells on the aspects of divine providence which seem to show God sifting and separating the lives of men. He stands for a rational reliance on the authority of the past (viii. 8 f.):

'Inquire, I pray thee, of the former age,
And apply thyself to that which their fathers have
  searched out:
(For we are but of yesterday and know nothing,
Because our days upon earth are a shadow :)
Shall they not teach thee and tell thee,
And utter words out of their heart?'

Against the 'I' of personal experience in the case of Eliphaz,
Bildad sets the 'we' of the fellowship of religious men.
Perhaps we may conceive him to be an anticipation of New-
man, drawn by his reason to reverence authority. Bildad
feels himself the heir of the ages; behind him in the past stands
the long line of men, whose treasured sayings are the library
of the present. He utters many proverbs and pointed sayings.
But he, too, like Eliphaz, is stirred to resentment at Job's
attitude, and bids him think of the darkened tent of the wicked,
when the last glimmer of the fire is dead, and the lamp has
burnt out (xviii. 5, 6).

Zophar is neither mystic nor traditionalist; he is what we
call to-day the man in the street, and for this reason we may
call him the Dogmatist. Of all men, the man in the street
is apt to be the most dogmatic; he repeats confidently what
he has neither tested by personal experience nor criticized by
reverent thought. If you point this out to the man in the street,
he is apt to get angry, like Zophar, who says the unkindest
thing in all this debate (xi. 6):

'Know therefore that God exacteth of thee less than thine
  iniquity deserveth.'

Zophar is silent in the last round; he could hardly have said
anything beyond this.

Elihu, who speaks with much self-confidence throughout
chapters xxxii-xxxvii, appears not to belong to the original
scheme of the poem, to which he contributes little. His
emphasis falls on affliction as discipline, to a more marked
degree than is the case with the others. He urges the sinful-
ness of Job's attitude, the prospect of restoration through

penitence, and the incomprehensible power of God. Most scholars are agreed that these chapters were inserted at some later date by a poet who wanted these points brought out more clearly. No reference is made to Elihu in either Prologue or Epilogue, and neither Job nor Yahweh notices him.

There can be no doubt that the object of the author, in the speeches of the three friends, was to show the inadequacy of contemporary doctrine to explain all suffering. In the three rounds of speeches, the friends successively point to the character of God, His government of the world, and the flaws in Job's past conduct which they infer from his present suffering. They fail utterly to solve his problem, and their point of view is explicitly condemned by Yahweh in the Epilogue. The reason for their failure is clear; they overlook some of the data for the solution of the problem, or even for understanding it. This world contains a vast amount of suffering which is unmerited; Job cannot explain it, but he does not wholly cease to believe that there is an explanation which does not dishonour God.

III

THE PROBLEM AS CREATED AND
HANDLED BY YAHWEH

WHAT, then, is the explanation of innocent suffering which
the writer of the Book of Job desired to offer, instead of the
falsely applied theory of the friends of Job? Since the author
does not speak in his own person, we shall naturally look for
this explanation in the utterances of Yahweh. The problem
of Job is brought into relation with Yahweh in three ways in
this Book. In the Epilogue we see Job restored to more than
his former prosperity. By the speeches delivered out of the
storm by Yahweh, His wisdow and power in Nature are
exhibited, and Job is brought to humble acknowledgment that
he cannot hope to understand all that Yahweh does. Finally,
the two incidents from the Council of Heaven given in the
Prologue reveal to the reader, *though not to Job*, the purpose
which Job's sufferings serve.

The first of these—the restoration of Job's fortunes—reads
like a child's tale. 'Yahweh gave Job twice as much as he
had before.' We can hardly help a smile at the quaint narrative of friendly calls and family festivals and congratulatory
gifts—'every man gave him a piece of money, and every one
a ring of gold.' We could do without his doubled number
of sheep and camels and oxen and she-asses; they only hide
from us the central figure, tragic, majestic, noble in his struggle,
but commonplace and comfortable in the last scene of all. We
do not want to know about his new daughters, with the
graceful names of Dove and Cassia and Horn of Antimony;
our sympathies are with the buried children of the earlier
days. We would rather have left Job on his dung-heap, with
faith shining the more brightly against the background of misfortune. This is the natural modern attitude, except for those
readers who want all tales to end happily, unlike the present

tale of life. But this is not the way to understand the Book of Job. We must remember that to the ancient readers of the Book there was no perspective of life beyond the grave, to which Job might look for the vindication of his faith. The ways of Providence must be justified, here in this world, if they are to be justified at all. It may be that this restoration is part of the traditional story of Job, which the writer has been content to reproduce. But he has accepted this vindication as necessary, by reproducing it, and from the point of view of his age he was right. The primary fact is that faith in God such as Job's must be justified; it is of secondary importance whether the justification come in the visible or in the invisible world. All that faith can demand is that, somewhere and somehow, he who throws himself upon God, whether perplexed or unperplexed, seeking, shall find Him.

Of more interest to us are the speeches of Yahweh contained in chapters xxxviii-xli. They have been truly described as 'the great poetical ornament of the Book,' 'the highest attainment of the Hebrew genius in pure poetry.' They fall into two distinct parts, the division of subject-matter in the first of the two speeches coming after xxxviii. 38. In the first part we have a brilliant description of natural phenomena—the subject-matter of the modern sciences of geology, physiography, meteorology and astronomy—of course from the ancient point of view, and with the ancient limitations of knowledge. The earth is a fixed, immovable building, which rests on solid foundations, and has all around it the sea. The sea is conceived in the spirit of ancient mythology as a giant, wrapped at birth in clouds and darkness for his swaddling-clothes and growing to strength till Yahweh has to restrain him. Every morning, with wonderful regularity, the dawn takes hold of the ends of the earth, and those who love darkness rather than light are shaken out of the earth's new garments of splendour. The earth, before hidden, stands revealed in all its detail, crisp and clear like the clay stamped by the seal. We are carried to the sources of the sea, the springs that keep up its supply, and down to the gates of the gloomy and cavernous Sheol that waits for all men. Yahweh keeps snow and hail piled in great storehouses above the solid firmament, armouries of his weapons for the day of battle. Light and wind and lightning have mysterious paths; the rain falls through a hole cut for it in the heavenly arch. We are bidden look at some of the familiar constellations, shining over Job as over us—the seven-starred sisterhood of the Pleiades, Orion the giant bound for his iniquities in heaven, the Great Bear swinging round by his tail. In the second part of Yahweh's utterance we review the animal world. The mighty lion, and the croaking raven, the wild goats and the hinds, the wild ass that scorns the tumult of the city, the unsubdued wild-ox, the ostrich that can outstrip the horse, the horse itself that smelleth the battle afar off, with the thunder of the captains and the shouting, the hawk migrating to the south, the eagle that sees from afar—all these pass before us, as a prelude to what forms the second speech of Yahweh—the account of the two wonderful creatures described in so much detail, the hippopotamus and the crocodile.[1]

A single purpose runs through both parts of this panorama of Nature. It is a sermon, all illustrations, on the text of God's wisdom and God's power. The application is to human ignorance and human weakness. If God does all this, how can men dare to criticize His administration of the Universe? The sermon is meant to teach Job humility, the cardinal virtue of religion. To some, perhaps, it seems a poor answer to tell Job that he cannot hope to understand the hidden purpose of God. Yet the revelation, however limited, which Nature affords, is a very real one. It has done its part if it teaches us the fear of the Lord that is the beginning of wisdom. 'What shall I answer Thee?' cries Job. 'Thou canst do all things.' 'I had heard of Thee by the hearing of the ear,'—that is according to the conventional theories of the age—'but now mine eye seeth Thee.' Thus Job admits the possibility of a wise, though hidden, purpose in his own sufferings.

We have now been brought as far towards the solution of the problem of innocent suffering as the author of the Book of Job intended his hero to be brought. Job has maintained

[1] Many scholars regard this second speech as a later addition to the book.

the conviction that suffering can befall an innocent man, a conviction which gives epoch-making significance to the Book. He has learnt that the tragedy of his life is not due to any neglect or moral imperfection in God, but to a divine purpose which passes beyond his understanding. Providence itself (as seen in the restored prosperity of the Epilogue) ultimately justifies the position for which he stands; for the rest, he has learnt the simple lesson of trust. But the author of the Book wants to take his readers a step further in the solution of the problem, beyond the lessons of Nature and the approvals of Providence. He does it by his picture of the Council of Heaven (i. 6-12, ii. 1-6), so strangely remote in form from our present conceptions of God, yet the parable of a truth which will carry us on into some of the deepest pages of the New Testament. Yahweh, like some Sultan of the East, sits on His throne above, surrounded by the angels, those ministers of His that do His pleasure. They come from all quarters, and one of them is the Satan, the Adversary. He is no fallen angel nor is he the Serpent of the Garden of Eden; this Book shows a prior stage in the history of his development. He is a regular member of the heavenly council, a sort of public prosecutor, bound to scrutinize every human claim to piety. It is true that his hand has been subdued to that it works in, like the dyer's hand; he is in process of becoming a Mephistopheles, a denying spirit (cf. Zech. iii. 1 ff.). Blake has made a fine contrast between the look of malignant joy on his face as he inflicts suffering on Job, and the look of sorrow on the face of Yahweh. But the Adversary's challenge of Job's piety is legitimate in principle. Yahweh has asked, 'Hast thou considered my servant Job?' The divine hand indicates him, brings him into a perilous prominence, saying, 'Here, if anywhere, is true piety.' The Adversary fixes attention on the other element in the combination—prosperity. Both the Satan and Yahweh agree in one point—in thinking that piety which depends on prosperity is not genuine. The Adversary alleges, and Yahweh denies, that this particular case of piety depends on prosperity. There can be but one way of settling this issue. The Adversary proposes, and receives permission, to remove all Job's prosperity. Accordingly, he robs Job first of all the

externals of life, without effect, and then almost of life itself.
This is the relation of the Adversary to Job; but Yahweh's
relation to him is much deeper. We have here no Miltonic
war between the Adversary and God. It is God who first calls
attention to Job, God who permits the trial of his faith, God
who watches the experiment, and assigns its proper limits.
Throughout, it is the will of God that is being done. The right
answer rings up from the earth when Job says: 'Shall we
receive good at the hand of God, and shall we not receive
evil?' All that comes to Job comes not by blind chance nor
by the compulsion of the Adversary. It is the simple development of God's first word: 'Hast thou considered my servant
Job?' There is a divine purpose in this innocent suffering,
other than retribution or discipline, for there is no hint that
Job is in need of either. That divine purpose is to prove to
angels and to men that disinterested religion is a reality and
that man can hold to God, not for what He gives, but for
Himself. This, then, is the fullest solution of the problem
of Job which the Book itself suggests to us, without, of course,
working out all that is implicit in the suggestion. We hear
an echo of its message across the centuries in Christ's answer
to the question: 'Master, who did sin, this man or his parents,
that he should be born blind?' The answer was, 'Neither did
this man sin nor his parents: but that the works of God should
be made manifest in him.' We see the same conception in-
spiring the Apostle Paul: 'I think God hath set forth us the
Apostles last of all, as men doomed to death, for we are made
a spectacle unto the world, both to angels and to men.' In
like manner, Job, as a gladiator of God, was made a spectacle
unto the world, both to angels and to men; led down into the
arena, as Paul's words suggest, and there bidden to fight for
the honour of God and the truth of piety. Some of the spectators who watched his struggle were visible to him; some were
not. A great cloud of witnesses for truth compassed him
about whilst he ran with patient impatience the race that was
set before him. With such a motive, such a purpose, had he
but known it, the race was worth running. He who can
realize something of what that purpose means will never say
of life:

We are here as on a darkling plain
Swept with confused alarms of struggle and flight,
Where ignorant armies clash by night.'

Is not this conception a real contribution to the problem of innocent suffering? Whenever a man can say in his heart, This calamity is not anything I have directly deserved, and when he can further say, I have learnt from this suffering all that I am able to learn, and yet it continues—then he is warranted in claiming for his own the great thought of the Book of Job, the thought that his suffering serves some larger purpose of God, such as the vindication of disinterested piety.[2] If we can really believe that, it gives us what we most need; it links our human lives with a divine purpose, just at the point where the purposes of God seem broken off. Pain is transformed into privilege; sorrow becomes the sign of God's approval. God trusts His servant—trusts him with the maintenance of eternal truths, trusts him to stand by them to the last. The trust is itself a reward, the reward of innocence, and the confirmation of piety, as much an honour as the sufferings of Plato's just man crucified. We often speak of trusting God; is there not often a neglected truth in the thought that God is trusting us?

[2] I am glad to see that this point is emphasized by Professor Hempel, in his *Althebräische Literatur* (1934), pp. 175-9. He represents Job as a true ' martyr ', i.e. a ' witness ' for God, whose intercession avails for his friends.

IV

THE PROBLEM IN RELATION
TO THE CHRISTIAN FAITH

THE Book of Job belongs to a great moral and religious development which culminated in the Christian faith. We have, then, finally to ask what is the Christian attitude towards the problem before us, the problem of innocent suffering? With the whole question of suffering we are, of course, not dealing. As penalty and as discipline—the two aspects of suffering urged by the friends of Job—suffering continues to be recognized by the Christian as by the Hebrew, but these aspects need not here concern us. It is clear enough that, in a moral world, evil which defies God and all His holy purposes must ultimately suffer; it is not less clear that a Father so wise as God will not spoil the children He loves by sparing the rod of chastening. But the Book of Job maintains that there is a large residue of unexplained suffering, and has offered an explanation of it, which we may provisionally call the maintenance of God's honour, and the witness to true religion. We have now to turn to the striking development of this idea which we find in the New Testament.

An important change has by this time come over the conditions of the problem. Job had no sure hope of immortality on which to rest the burden of his problem. All must be solved within this world, if ever. Now, within the period lying between the Old Testament and the New, there grew up in Judaism (partly from such beginnings as those made by Job), a strong faith in life after death, a life in which the arrears of moral retribution left over from this world were balanced up. Men turned from their national misfortunes to the individual hope of immortality, or rather, of resurrection. They endured their undeserved sorrows, because they believed that to them as individuals, if not to them as a nation, Yahweh would return double for all their shame. They could die in this faith, because the perspective of life was lengthened beyond death, and the adjustment would come there if not here. This faith in a future life was current in Judaism when our Lord began His mission; He took it and lifted it to a higher spiritual level by giving it a richer content. He taught that a man might well fling down his life here, in the prospect of finding it there. The life after death as He set it forth gave scope for the ample working out of such spiritual laws as those of the Beatitudes.

All this, however, simply extends the life man lives; whereas the Christian faith, apart altogether from immortality, has welcomed innocent suffering into its very heart. It has taken the world's sorrow and given it the possibility of a new meaning, a transfigured purpose. By common consent, at the historic centre of Christianity, there is the Cross, and the Cross means innocent suffering, serving a divine purpose. Men differ in the interpretation of that purpose, as they did in Job's day, and there are views of it no better than those of Job's friends. But in some way that purpose is held to be redemptive and vital to Christianity. It is not the Sermon on the Mount, but the Cross of Calvary which is the centre of our faith, and Jesus would never have become the World-Teacher He is if He had not been first and foremost a World-Saviour. Does the Cross of Job, then, throw any light on the Cross of Christ, and that which His disciples bear after Him?

First, we have to note that this innocent Sufferer made the endurance of innocent suffering one of the absolutely necessary conditions of discipleship. In the most solemn circumstances, after Peter's declaration of His Messiahship, and His own of His approaching death, He called the multitudes to Him, and said to them and to the disciples: " If any man would come after me, let him deny himself, and take up his cross and follow me." Here are three requirements, viz., self-renunciation, acceptance of innocent suffering, and obedient imitation. No man is a full disciple of Christ, according to His own statement, unless these three are being fulfilled, and the three are really one—the acceptance of the principle of the Cross. The figure of taking up the Cross is drawn from the all too common spectacle of the time—that of the condemned slave going to

the place of execution and forced to carry his own gallows.
It is a strong figure, purposely chosen to set the truth in its
clearest form. It does not include all suffering, but only that
suffering which is encountered in the definite way of discipleship. Cross-bearing in Christ's sense does not mean petty
annoyances or the results of our own follies or sins. It means
a certain fellowship in innocent suffering with Himself. It
supplies a central principle of Christian ethics, the principle
of victory through defeat. The Royal Way of the Holy Cross,
as à Kempis called it, is the great high-road of the Kingdom on
which the King is best proclaimed, and loyalty to the King is
formed and tested. Surely William Penn was right in the book
written in prison, *No Cross, No Crown,* when he said:

'We must either renounce to believe what the Lord Jesus
hath told us, that whosoever doth not bear his cross and come
after Him cannot be His disciple, or admitting that for truth,
conclude that [the] generality of Christendom do miserably
deceive and disappoint themselves in the great business of
Christianity and their own salvation.' The Christian, then, is
called to carry the Cross of disinterested piety, like Job and a
greater than Job.

But there is an even deeper aspect of both the Cross of Christ
and the cross-bearing of His disciples, to which the Book of
Job points the way. To understand it, we must recall the purpose for which that Book was written. It was written after
the Jewish Exile, when the national spirit was almost broken,
and the innocent suffered with the guilty all the sorrows of a
forced migration, and of its attendant evils. Israel's proud
consciousness of a divine mission was almost destroyed; the
nation could no more hope to tread the path of victory. At
that crisis came the great Prophet of the Exile, whom we call
Deutero-Isaiah, with his confidence in Israel's restoration. But
instead of the old ideal of national supremacy, he sketched, in
the figure of the Suffering Servant of Yahweh, a new ministry
to the world. Israel was to be a Man of Sorrows—at least all
those who entered into Israel's ideal were to be this—acquainted
with grief. Israel's sorrows were to be an offering for sin. The
righteous Servant of Yahweh bears the sin of many and makes
intercession for the transgressors—even for those who despised

and rejected the Sufferer, and hid their faces from Him. Let us think of the companion figure of Job belonging to approximately the same period, though probably somewhat later, and dealing with the same problem, though in a different way. Job, also, was rejected by his friends; yet Job, too, is bidden to pray for those who shall be accepted for his sake. There are so many parallels between the figure of the Servant of Yahweh and the figure of Job that some have seen in Job's case also a reference to the national fortunes of Israel, and the great problem of Israel's sufferings as a nation. But the innocent suffering which the Prophet of the Exile conceives as an offering for sin, the author of the Book of Job interprets as a vindication of disinterested religion, and of God's honour. It was through such thoughts as these, and along both lines of interpretation, that our Lord entered into the consciousness of his mission. He clearly identified Himself in the synagogue at Nazareth with the Servant of Yahweh. Is is too much to say also that the cup which His Father held to his lips He drank in the attitude of Job—an attitude the more like Job's because of the moment of doubt, 'My God, my God, why hast thou forsaken me?'

If we come to the Cross of Christ, and to the doctrine of Atonement which gathers round it, from this point of view, we shall escape all those merely transactional ideas of the death of Christ which degrade its holy mystery. Great and wise men have conceived the Atonement in many different ways. Augustine, for example, thought of the death of Christ as a ransom paid to the devil. Anselm conceived it as the payment of a debt we had incurred by our sins and could not possibly pay ourselves. The Reformers thought of it as the penalty for sin, the punishment we ought to have borne, which Christ bore in our stead. Grotius held it to be a manifestation of the righteousness of God's public government, that sin should not be overlooked. I do not want to question the element of truth in even the worst of these figures and metaphors. I believe that the history of religion without, and the demands of conscience within, show the need for a deeper Atonement for sin than the simple change of attitude in the sinful will of God's rebellious children. But I am sure that many, who feel this, are repelled by some of the traditional ways of stating it; whereas the Book of Job might supply a way of approach to the interpretation of the Cross which would remove all such stumbling-blocks. We have seen that the Book teaches God's permission of innocent suffering for an end that justifies it, and that Job, by his disinterested piety, fulfilled that end. Now let us try to lift our thought to something vaster, something far more wonderful than those Councils of Heaven which are the key to Job's fortunes. Let us think of the Son of God, the first-born among many brethren, entering this world as Jesus of Nazareth, because God so loved the world, and the Son so loved it for the Father's sake. Let us think of God looking out on the cosmic harvest, the fields white with the souls of men, and seeing that sin was spoiling the result—seeing that even if all men turned at last to Him there would remain a sinful record, the long story of dishonour to God running through human history. God's honour was at stake as by the Adversary's challenge; His purpose in creating the world would be defeated if the world's worth to Him were not realized, in disinterested piety. God's way of making the world worth while to Himself is a very wonderful one, for it is a double victory over sin. He does not simply send into the world a Prophet who shall turn men from evil to good, He sends a Saviour whose innocent suffering shall atone for that long sinful past. Jesus atones by His personal vindication of that Kingdom of God which is disinterested piety, by His intercession for those who have added to His sufferings to the Father, in fulfilment of a purpose partly hidden from His human consciousness.[1] In each respect Job was His forerunner, and all these things are true of Jesus as a man, just as they were true of Job. But the Christian faith is not content to regard Jesus as merely a man, or even as the highest of men. It sees in Him God manifest in the flesh, so that what is true of the man who is seen must be in some sense true of the God who is not seen. The Gospel declares that God vindicated His own cause by entering the world through His Son, and through His Cross bears the burden of the suffering caused by the sin of man, and by the grace of this sin-bearing, both in Jesus

[1] This seems to me the inevitable inference from Mark xiv. 36; xv. 34.

and in all in whom the Spirit of God is, makes the world with all its sin a more glorious place than would have been a world of innocence without sin.[2] Christ is like a Rock—we call Him the Rock of Ages—on which a dark wave breaks, and is broken into countless fragments, bright in the sunshine. The wave of sin breaks on Him, and He conquers it, by making it a new manifestation of divine grace. He does all this by the suffering He must face in order to bring these realities into a sinful world. The Cross is the price of divine entrance into a world of sin. Christ paid that price (to speak in metaphor), that He might redeem the world. His own realization of the supreme values of personality is not only a moral influence on man, but also a redemptive offering to God. In prospect it achieves the end of cosmic evolution in the creation of holy personality; in retrospect, it enriches an impoverished world with the worth of God, the utterly disinterested piety of Him who is not less the incarnate God because He is the perfect man.

This approach to the Atonement suggests the close relation of Christ's Cross to the cross-bearing on which He insisted for His disciples. In the apostle's words, they 'fill up that which is lacking of the afflictions of Christ in [their] flesh for His body's sake, which is the Church', they are 'poured out as a drink-offering upon the sacrifice and service of the faith' of others. These words must mean that in some real sense the Christian life is always and everywhere an offering to God, which realizes that for which Christ died. Each of us, in whom the Spirit of Christ is, is continuing Christ's work of lifting the world, for it is He who works within us. He has made Atonement for us all; we can rest securely in the grace of God displayed in and assured by Christ. But just so far as we are brought into a living union with that grace of Atonement, we must needs experience the energy of a new indwelling Spirit. Within the great solidarity of the race, which makes it impossible for any man to live his life apart, without finding life not worth living, there is the solidarity of the Christian company, sharing in the great two-fold work

[2] For a fuller treatment of this theme, see my essay on 'The Christian Gospel of Redemption', in The Christian Faith, edited by W. R. Matthews (Eyre and Spottiswoode, 1936).

done by the innocent suffering of Christ. They help to vindicate disinterested piety; they humbly share in the mystery of the world's redemption. The proof that they share in the benefits of Christ's suffering is that they share its spirit, and are ready to endure it in their own lives. So we find innocent suffering carried on from the animal world, where it seems to be the necessary price of progress, in a vast evolution up to man. But, on the level of human personality, the suffering fulfils a new function, by becoming consciously vicarious, after the pattern and under the influence of Christ's.

The Book of Job is, in this sense, a first draft of the Gospel story, for it shows a man who bore his cross before Christ; not uncomplaining, for the burden of a mystery was upon him which can never be on us to the same degree since the Cross of Christ, yet bravely and truly, so as, by what he suffered, to enrich the world in God's eyes as well as man's. It shows us one who fulfilled a large and divine purpose in thus bearing the Cross, a purpose extending far beyond his horizon, a purpose which appeals to us to-day, as we are made spectators of the Cross of Job. It proclaims the truth, afterwards to be taken up into the Christian Gospel, that the suffering of the innocent can have a cosmic purpose, nobler than the height of any of our explanations.[3] It supplies a new conception of life, in thus meeting one of its sorest problems. It does all this, because of the courage and sincerity of that unknown author, who gave us what he must first have learnt in suffering before he could teach it in song. It moves us to-day—I know one man, at least, to whom it has been an Old Testament Gospel, opening its message to him first in a time of much trouble—it moves us to-day because it is so loyal to life, with all life's broken ends and tangled skein, so loyal to our highest faith that all broken ends will be re-knit and all entanglements at last unravelled.

[3] In the approach to the subject from the parallel experience of Jeremiah (in 'The Cross of Jeremiah', pp. 181 ff.) I have indicated the bearing of this on the doctrine of divine suffering.

II

THE CROSS OF THE SERVANT

PREFACE

THIS little book on a great subject consists of three lectures delivered at the Regent's Park College Summer School of 1926, under the Angus Lectureship Trust. In general, it can claim to be no more than a very elementary introduction to a theme on which a whole library has been written. But in two respects it opens up less familiar ground, to which the attention of more advanced students may be usefully directed. One is the employment of the ancient idea of corporate personality to elucidate the conception of the Servant, and the further application of this idea to the New Testament conception of the Body of Christ. The other is the new interpretation offered of Philippians ii. 7, according to which 'He emptied Himself' is derived from Isaiah liii. 12, 'He poured out his soul unto death,' and therefore refers to the Cross, rather than to the Incarnation.

The purpose of the book continues that of *The Cross of Job* and *The Cross of Jeremiah*, in which I have tried to show the deep underlying unities of the Bible, yet more explicit in the present subject. It is no rhetorical exaggeration, but sober truth in the light of criticism, history and psychology, to describe the Songs of the Servant as the Old Testament portrait of Jesus Christ.

The book has been read in typescript by Professors G. H. Box and H. T. Andrews, and in proof by Professor A. J. D. Farrer, and I have to thank all these friends for their useful criticisms.

H. WHEELER ROBINSON

Regent's Park College
London N.W.8

' AND at his [the unjust man's] side let us place the just man in his noble-
ness and simplicity, wishing, as Aeschylus says, to be and not to seem
good. There must be no seeming, for if he seem to be just he will be
honoured and rewarded, and then we shall not know whether he is just
for the sake of justice or for the sake of honours and rewards; therefore,
let him be clothed in justice only, and have no other covering; and he must
be imagined in a state of life the opposite of the former. Let him be the
best of men, and let him be thought the worst; then he will have been
put to the proof; and we shall see whether he will be affected by the fear
of infamy and its consequences. And let him continue thus to the hour of
death; being just and seeming to be unjust . . . the just man who is thought
unjust will be scourged, racked, bound—will have his eyes burnt out; and,
at last, after suffering every kind of evil, he will be impaled.'

Plato, The Republic, Bk. II. (361) (Jowett's translation in
The Dialogues of Plato, III., pp. 40, 41).

Let us see if his words be true,
And let us try what shall befall in the ending of his life.
For if the righteous man is God's son, he will uphold him,
And he will deliver him out of the hand of his adversaries.
With outrage and torture let us put him to the test,
That we may learn his gentleness,
And may prove his patience under wrong.
Let us condemn him to a shameful death;
For he shall be visited according to his words. . . .

But the souls of the righteous are in the hand of God,
And no torment shall touch them.
In the eyes of the foolish they seemed to have died;
And their departure was accounted to be their hurt,
And their journeying away from us to be their ruin :
But they are in peace.
For even if in the sight of men they be punished,
Their hope is full of immortality;
And having borne a little chastening, they shall receive great good;
Because God made trial of them, and found them worthy of himself.
As gold in the furnace he proved them,
And as a whole burnt offering he accepted them.'

The Wisdom of Solomon, ii. 17-iii. 6.

CONTENTS

2. The Jewish interpretation of the suffering of the Servant.

The Servant not the Messiah; no pre-Christian doctrine of a suffering Messiah; the later Judaism interprets the Servant as Israel.

The national suffering of Israel, especially in the Middle Ages.

The attitude of the finer spirits within Israel towards such suffering (Judah ha-Levi).

The group of Maccabean martyrs and their offering for the nation (development of individualism).

III. THE MESSIAH-SERVANT   98

The actuality of the suffering to be interpreted.

1. The influence of the portrait of the Servant upon the consciousness of Jesus :

(1) The voice at the Baptism.

(2) His acceptance of death as part of His mission.

(3) The ransom and covenant-blood, shed for many.

2. The general identification of the Servant with Jesus within the New Testament.

3. The collective aspect of the Servant continued (in fact) by the corporate consciousness of the Church :

(1) The Ecclesia as the new Israel.

(2) The 'fellowship' of the Ecclesia.

4. The permanent value of the approach to that Atonement through the Servant:

Recognition of :

(1) The reality of history.

(2) The corporate unity of the Church and its Head.

(3) The permanent place of sacrifice in the forgiveness of sin.

THE SONGS OF THE SERVANT

I. THE PATIENT TEACHER OF TRUE RELIGION TO ALL
(Isaiah xlii. 1-4)

(Yahweh speaks)

> Lo! my servant, whom I uphold,
>   My chosen, the joy of my heart;
> I have given my spirit upon him,
>   Religion for the nations shall he bring forth.
>
> Nor crying aloud, nor lifting his voice,
>   Nor making it heard out of doors—
> No crushed reed will he break off,
>   No dim-burning wick will he quench.
>
> Faithfully will he bring forth religion,
>   Himself undimmed and unbroken,
> Till he set religion in the earth,
>   And the shores shall look for his teaching.

II. THE DIVINE EQUIPMENT AND WORLD-MISSION OF THE SERVANT
(Isaiah xlix. 1-6)

(The Servant speaks)

> Hearken to me, ye shores,
>   Attend, ye peoples, from afar;
> Yahweh has called me from the womb,
>   From my mother's body recorded my name;
>
> Made my mouth a sharpened sword,
>   Hid me in the shade of His hand;
> He made me a polished arrow,
>   In His quiver He stored me;
>
> Saying, 'My servant are thou,
>   By whom I will get me glory';
> So was I honoured in Yahweh's eyes,
>   And my God became my strength.
>
> I, indeed, said, 'In vain have I toiled,
>   Spent my strength for airy nought';
> But surely my right is with Yahweh,
>   My wages are with my God.

61

And now 'tis Yahweh's purpose,
　　Who shaped me from birth for His servant,
To restore Jacob to Himself,
　　Gathering Israel unto Him.

'Too slight' (he said) 'to raise Jacob's tribes,
　　And to restore the survivors of Israel;
So I give thee a light of nations,
　　That my saving work be to earth's end.'

III. THE SERVANT'S SUFFERING AND CONFIDENCE IN THE DISCHARGE OF HIS MISSION
(Isaiah l. 4-9)

(The Servant speaks)

The Lord Yahweh has given me
　　The tongue of disciples,
To know how to speak
　　A word in due season;

At morn wakening my ear,
　　To hear like disciples;
And *I* have not rebelled,
　　Backward have I not turned.

My back I gave to smiters,
　　My cheeks to torturers;
My face I did not hide
　　From shameful spitting.

And the Lord Yahweh will help me,
　　Therefore am I not ashamed,
But have set my face as a flint,
　　And I know that I shall not be shamed.

Near is my justifier,
　　Who will contend with me?
　　　　Let us stand up together;
Who is my adversary?
　　Let him draw near to me.

Lo! the Lord Yahweh will help me,
　　Who is he that will convict me?
Lo! they shall all perish as a garment,
　　Moth shall devour them.

IV. THE SERVANT'S VICARIOUS SUFFERING; HIS PAST HUMILIATION AND FUTURE VINDICATION
(Isaiah lii.13-liii. 12)

(Yahweh speaks)

Lo! my servant shall prosper,
　　Shall be high and greatly exalted;

As many were astounded at him,
  So shall many nations tremble,
    Kings will be silent before him;
For what was not told them have they seen,
  And what they have not heard have they discerned:—

(*The nations speak*)

  Who would have believed what we hear,
    And to whom was Yahweh's arm revealed?
  For he grew up before Him as a sapling,
    And as a root from dry ground.

  No form had he that we should look at him,
    No appearance that we should delight in him;
  So destroyed from manhood his aspect,
    And his form from the sons of men.

  Despised and forsaken by men,
    A man of pains and familiar with sickness:
  As one from whom faces are hidden,
    Despised was he and unvalued.

  But surely our sicknesses *he* bore,
    And our pains—he carried them;
  Whilst *we* thought him stricken,
    Smitten and afflicted by God.

  But *he* was pierced through our rebellions,
    Crushed through our iniquities;
  The chastisement bringing us welfare was on him,
    And by the stripes he bore there was healing for us.

  All of us like sheep had wandered,
    Each of us turning his own way,
  But Yahweh made fall on him,
    The iniquity of all of us.

  He was hard pressed, and let himself be humbled,
    Nor opened he his mouth;
  As a sheep that is led to slaughter,
    And as a ewe before her shearers is dumb.

  Through oppression his right was taken away,
    And who gave heed to his dwelling?
  For he was cut off from the land of the living,
    Through the rebellion of the peoples was he smitten to death.

  And they gave him his grave with the wicked,
    And with evil-doers when he died;
  Though he had done no violence,
    And deceit was not in his mouth.

But Yahweh willed to cleanse him from his sickness
    (If ye make his life a trespass-offering,
    He shall see a seed that prolongs its days),
And Yahweh's will was to deliver him from trouble;
    He shall see light and be satisfied with his knowledge.

(Yahweh speaks)

My servant shall justify many,
    And their iniquities *he* shall bear;
Therefore he shall inherit with the great,
    And with the mighty divide the spoil;

Because he emptied out his life to death,
    And with the rebellious let himself be numbered;
But *he* bore the sin of many,
    And interposed for the rebellious.

CRITICAL NOTES (for which reference should be made to the verse-notation
of the R.V.)
    xlix. 3: 'Israel' has been added in M.T.; cf. LXX of xlii. 1.
    xlix. 5: Words within brackets of R.V. should follow xlix. 3.
    xlix. 6: M.T. inserts 'for thee to be my servant'.
    l. 4: M.T. 'to help (?) the weary with a word'; text doubtful. M.T.
has a dittograph in 4, and a paraphrase in 5.
    l. 6: literally, 'to pluckers-out' (of hair).
    l. 7: LXX 'But'; M.T. 'Therefore'.
    lii. 13: M.T. adds, 'and raised up'.
    lii. 14: so Versions; M.T. 'at thee'. Second part of verse seems to belong
after liii. 2.
    lii. 15: LXX suggests 'tremble'; M.T. 'be startled" (?).
    liii. 2: M.T. adds 'and no honour'.
    liii. 7: M.T. repeats 'nor opened he his mouth'.
    liii. 8: by transposition of one letter, 'and judgment' becomes 'his right'.
    liii. 8: so partly LXX; but M.T. 'my people' must be wrong, since the
nations are speaking.
    liii. 9: M.T. has 'the rich' for 'evil-doers'.
    liii. 10, 11: very confused; all translations are conjectural, with a little
help from the versions.
    liii. 11: 'righteous' seems to be a dittograph.

(M.T.=the Massoretic, i.e. the standard Hebrew, text;
LXX=the Septuagint, i.e. the ancient Greek Version.)

I

WHO WAS THE SERVANT OF YAHWEH?

IT is a striking comment on both the transience and the permanence of human life that the world's most famous literary portrait should be one of an uncertain subject, executed by an unknown hand. The transience—but did Isaiah of Babylon desire to be anything more than a voice crying in the wilderness? The permanence—for when once Spirit has achieved articulate expression in some notable form, its lineaments fascinate and arrest us by some intrinsic right. It is as though we were passing along the picture-gallery of a great house, the creation and shrine of a noble lineage, and amongst all the portraits of distinguished ancestors, bearing the names of well-known artists, there was one that had no label, one of tragic mien as well as of perplexing anonymity, yet one which stood out from all the rest by its inherent right, and compelled our testimony, 'Surely, this was the greatest of them all.' The greatest figure in the portrait-gallery of the Old Testament is an unsolved enigma. There are great kings there, like David, of whom we know even the intimate details of family and court life, the human passions beneath the royal robe, the meanness of lust, the generosity of comradeship; there are great prophets there, like Jeremiah, who has bared his own heart that we may see God through it; there are great poet-thinkers, like the author of the Book of Job, who wrestle with the mystery of divine providence and human destiny. But none of these, for all their greatness, has the ultimate religious significance of the Servant of Yahweh. Yet who is he? The prophet himself, a 'self-portrait' such as painters have often executed? or some historical figure of his own or a past age, as to whom we are left to conjecture dimly and speculatively? or some mystery-god, the spoil of the Gentiles, appropriated by Israel? Or is he none of these, but the individualized portrait

65   E

of a group, the composite photograph of a community? and if so, is that community Israel, or some particular association within it? and if Israel, is it Israel after the flesh or after the spirit, the real or the ideal nation?

All these views have been defended by competent Old Testament scholars, and the literature of the subject is enormous—so great, indeed, that a well-known commentator is said to have abandoned his projected commentary on Isaiah because this part of his subject overwhelmed him. The variety of views reminds us that the problem is complex and subtle, and this fact should check a superficial dogmatism. But the problem presented to historical exegesis, fascinating and important as it is, must not be confused with the larger issues for theology. Every student must make up his mind on the balance of evidence as to the identification of the portrait. Yet, whatever be that identification, the religious ideas involved in it will claim our primary attention. The cardinal fact for the Christian student is that to those ideas Jesus of Nazareth has served Himself heir, and He has blended the details of its portrait with His own. This fact alone is sufficient to make ' the fifty-third of Isaiah ' the most important page of the Old Testament for the student of the New. But, since He whom Christians serve is acclaimed by them as the Truth, they are bound to seek diligently for the historical truth of words and ideas which came to mean so much to their Lord.

1. We have said, ' the fifty-third of Isaiah,' because this is the most impressive portion of the poems describing the Suffering Servant. But this chapter has been quite artificially and wrongly separated from the last three verses of the previous chapter, without which it cannot be understood. Further, there are three other poems which evidently belong to the same cycle, and, in the judgment of most scholars, lead up to this culminating point. The first of these is found in Isaiah xlii. 1-4, and describes the Servant as chosen and upheld by Yahweh, spiritually endowed for his mission of a quiet, patient and persistent proclamation of true religion to the ends of the earth. The second is found in xlix. 1-6, in which we hear the Servant himself speaking to all men. Yahweh has predestined him from birth for his mission, and has equipped him with a powerful

message. If for a moment the toil seems vain, there is renewal of strength in the thought that his interests are God's, whose purpose is not simply to restore a scattered Israel, but to make his Servant a light of all the nations. The third poem is found in l. 4-9, where the Servant again speaks. He learns his message from God, and has not been unfaithful in its delivery. But this has brought upon him shame and suffering, though he can confidently rest his cause on God. The fourth and longest poem (lii. 13-liii. 12) resembles the first in form, for Yahweh again speaks to declare the overwhelming surprise of His Servant's final triumph, a surprise acknowledged by the kings of the nations, who are overwhelmed with astonishment. There had been nothing in the previous history of the Servant to prepare them for this, for he had been despised and forsaken of men. But now they see a hidden meaning in his sufferings, which have been endured not for his own sin, but for the healing of others. That which he has borne was really their due, yet he submitted quietly even to actual death. In the issue Yahweh restores him to life, and his vicarious suffering brings him to glory and honour. Such is the argument of the four poems, of which the progressive unity is apparent.

The four 'Songs of the Servant of Yahweh' are now embedded in a collection of prophetic poems extending from the fortieth to the fifty-fifth chapter of our Book of Isaiah. These chapters can be assigned with confidence to the period of Israel's exile in Babylon, for they pre-suppose its conditions, and promise a speedy deliverance from them. Not only so, but they definitely point to the instrument and manner of that deliverance. It was about the middle of the sixth century that the brilliant career of Cyrus began. He was originally a vassal of Media, which he mastered in 549. He then led the united Medes and Persians to the conquest of Asia Minor, and finally, after subduing the surrounding peoples, to that of Babylon in 539. At some time, then, within this decade (549-539), the eye of the unknown prophet-poet was arrested by this Napoleonic figure of Cyrus, and his mouth was inspired to hail him as the 'anointed' of Yahweh (xlv. 1), divinely commissioned to overthrow Babylon and to restore Israel to Palestine. In a series of more or less detached, but congruous poems, Deutero-

Isaiah (as we may conveniently call the author) bids his fellow-exiles to cherish the highest hopes that they will soon be free and gloriously restored to their own land.   He rests his case on the power of Yahweh, the great Creator, over all nature (xl. 12f.) and all history (xli. 2f.).   Yahweh alone knows and reveals the future (xli. 21-29).   What folly it is to worship dumb idols (xliv. 9f.)!

It will be seen that the general theme of these other poems is distinct from, though not inconsistent with, the theme of the Songs of the Servant.   Broadly speaking, the other poems are a call to hope, whilst these are a picture of service rendered through suffering.   If we ask what is the present relation of these Songs of the Servant to their immediate context, the answer is not easy, because of the general character of such prophetic writings, which resemble an anthology rather than a sustained literary effort.   It is possible that the Songs of the Servant were not originally found in their present context; but if so, they would seem to have been inserted by their author or editor with some relation to it, perhaps on the view that the Servant is Israel.   This, of course, would still leave open the question of the original intention of these Songs, as it would that of authorship.   We know that Jeremiah adapted earlier oracles of his own, dealing with the Scythian advance, to the much later Babylonian invasion; Deutero-Isaiah or a collector of his poems might have incorporated two cycles of poems distinct in their origin.   But if we could assert with confidence identity of authorship, then we should have a very powerful argument for maintaining that the picture of the Servant in the Songs is really a picture of Israel, for there is no doubt that in the other poems the title 'Servant' is given to Israel as a people.

2. The term denoting 'Servant' does not, in itself, carry us far for our present purpose.   It is naturally a term of very wide range, from the slave who was sold into a foreign land (Gen. xxxix. 17) up to a court official or minister of state (2 Kings xxii. 12; *cf.* Gen. xl. 20).   As applied to the worshippers of God, its range is not less wide, for it can be used both of the rank and file and of the prophets of Yahweh (2 Kings ix. 7; cf. Ps. xxxiv. 22 and Jer. vii. 25).   Clearly the

title is one of honour when we find it applied to Abraham,
Isaac and Jacob (Deut. ix. 27), Moses (Deut. xxxiv. 5), Joshua
(Josh. xxiv. 29), David (Ps. xviii., title), Isaiah (Isa. xx. 3), and
Job i. 8). Since it was according to the Hebrew custom to
designate a people by the name of some ancestor, such as Israel
or Jacob, we can see how easy was the transition to speaking
of the people Israel as the servant, instead of 'the servants'
of Yahweh. Thus Jeremiah says, 'Fear thou not, O Jacob
my servant, saith Yahweh; neither be dismayed, O Israel:
for, lo, I will save thee from afar, and thy seed from the land
of their captivity; and Jacob shall return' (xxx. 10). A striking
example of this collective use of the term 'servant' may be
found in Ezekiel xxxvii. 25, where it is said that 'my servant
David' shall be king over the land of 'Jacob my servant', the
first term and possibly the second denoting not an individual,
but a group—the succession of princes of Davidic blood and
the succession of people of Israelite stock. This use of the
term is frequent in Deutero-Isaiah: 'Israel my servant, Jacob
whom I have chosen' (xli. 8; cf. xliv. 1, 21, xlv. 4); 'Yahweh
hath redeemed his servant Jacob' (xlviii. 20). As a title of
honour, the term certainly denotes the religious relation of
devotion (cf. the name Abdullah=the servant of Allah), and
may also include the sense of a special mission,[1] as in the words
'Ye are my witnesses, saith Yahweh, and my servant whom I
have chosen' (xliii. 10). On the other hand, there is a striking
passage which dwells on the faults of Israel as Yahweh's servant: 'Hear, ye deaf: and look, ye blind, that ye may see.
Who is blind, but my servant? or deaf, as my messenger that
I send?' (xlii. 18, 19).

In the light of such passages, there would be a strong pre-
sumption that the term 'Servant' in the four songs is used
there also of Israel in the collective sense, if we could assume
identity of authorship. Apart from this assumption, all we
are warranted in saying so far is that the previous usage of
the term leaves it an open question whether 'Servant' denotes
an individual or a group. But we must not allow the term
'Servant' to suggest of necessity anything lowly and humble
in place. We are left free, therefore, by the use of the term

[1] Cheyne, *Ency. Bib.*, col. 4400.

' Servant ' to recognize the direct evidence of the Songs, that
the Servant is a figure not only of national but of international
importance, with whom the kings of the nations must reckon.
No obscure and private person could have been the Servant
intended by the prophet, and those who seek an individual
reference have not yet discovered with any unanimity any
prominent and public personage of this age adequate to the
effect on the world described in the Songs. On the other hand,
if the Servant is Israel as a people, we have at once a real
entity of international importance, at least in the eyes of a
prophet. It is no longer disproportionate to suggest that the
remarkable restoration of the Servant to his old position and
more would be likely to make a deep impression on the surrounding peoples and their kings.

3. What, then, are the obstacles in the way of identifying
the Servant in these four Songs with the people of Israel?
We may be sure that there are real difficulties, for otherwise
the opposition to it would not have been so persistent, so
varied, and so supported by scholarly arguments. It is not
practicable to enter on any detailed discussion of these arguments; it will be sufficient to say that they turn on two cardinal
points, viz. (*1*) the general impression made on the reader that
the portrait is too special and elaborate in its details to represent any group of men, and must have been drawn from an
individual ' sitter ', whether a historical personage such as
Jeremiah or the typical representative of a class or of an idea;
and (2) the fact that more than once in the present text of
the Songs a real distinction seems to be made between the
work of the Servant and the national life as its sphere of operation. These two difficulties must be frankly faced, if we are
to know how far they can be adequately met.

The elements which suggest that the portrait is one of an
individual are to be found in all the four Songs, though they
are most marked in the fourth. In the first, we are led to
think of the gentleness and patience of a definite character,
the very opposite of the noisy and tyrannical demeanour of a
world-conqueror. In the second, we are shown his subjective
reaction to apparent failure, and his personal reassertion of a
challenged faith—the familiar story of any man who strives to

realize his ideals in a materialistic world. In the third, we seem to be carried deeper into the understanding of this situation, both on its inner and its outer side. On the inner side, this protagonist for divine truth tells us that he is sustained by personal communion with God, his constant teacher. Because of that communion he is able to endure both physical and spiritual pain; his 'head is bloody but unbowed'; his persistent purpose to obey God is flint-like in its strength. Again we recognize the truth to actual life of such traits; opposition always strengthens where it does not overthrow. He has real and powerful enemies, but he is sure that Yahweh is greater than all of them. In the fourth Song, we are told the story of a human life, obscure in origin, unattractive in appearance, burdened by sickness, solitary and misunderstood, a life brought at last to patient death and ignominious burial— yet a life destined to issue in a glorious resurrection and an ample vindication of its fine nobility of unselfish purpose. As we reflect on the particularity and definiteness of all these features, and note their essential unity, we are bound to admit that this is either a portrait from actual life or a great work of creative imagination. We feel that we should know this man if we met him, or at least that he is such a man as we might actually meet, by some rare privilege of human intercourse.

Such, I say, is the impression made by the Songs upon us, especially upon us Westerns and moderns, when we try to bring an impartial judgment to their study. But before we are justified in inferring that no community could be 'averaged out' in such wealth of personal detail, let us remember that we are reading a Semitic and Oriental book, written when life was much more concrete and picturesque, and by people to whom our abstract methods of thought and presentation were impossible. Fortunately for us, they could not discuss sociological or historical or religious problems with our own wealth —or poverty—of long words; to utter a general truth at all, they had to use the particular image. Like the Rabbis in the Mishnah, who discuss the general case through the particular example, or like Jesus in His parable of the Good Samaritan, who defines sociality by telling the story of the man whose humanity was deeper than his nationality, the writers of the

Old Testament have the Semitic genius for detail, and the Semitic weakness in generalization. In prophecy, this unconscious racial tendency was wedded to conscious poetic imagination. So when Isaiah of Jerusalem would describe the social conditions of his time, and analyse their moral and religious factors, he instinctively describes an individual figure :

> ' The whole head is sick,
>   And the whole heart diseased :
> From the sole of the foot to the very head
>   No soundness is in him;
> (But) bruises and contusions
>   And still bleeding wounds,
> Not pressed out, nor bound up,
>   Nor softened with oil.'
>
>   (Isa. i. 5, 6; Gray's trans.)

There is no hint in that stanza that anyone but a single person is meant, yet the context shows clearly that the portrait is of Israel the nation. It may be granted that the fourth Servant Song is much more sustained and elaborate in its working out of such a portrait, yet is it essentially different in character from this other portrait of a sick man, in spite of the very different application of the portrait? Or take the familiar example of the one hundred-and-twenty-ninth Psalm :

> ' Many a time have they afflicted me from my youth up :
> Yet they have not prevailed against me.
> The plowers ploughed upon my back :
> They made long their furrows.
> Yahweh is righteous :
> He hath cut asunder the cords of the wicked.'

Those words at once suggest the third of the Servant Songs in its most individualized features :

> ' I gave my back to the smiters,
> And my cheeks to them that plucked off my hair :
> I hid not my face from shame and spitting ' (Isa. l. 6).

But the parallel in the Psalm is expressly assigned to Israel—
'Let Israel now say.' The most impressive example of Hebrew
particularism, for our present purpose, may be found in the
work of Deutero-Isaiah himself—his portrait of Zion, which
familiarity leads us to dismiss too easily as mere metaphor.
The portrait of Zion is relatively as fully individualized as that
of the Servant of Yahweh, though we never question the fact
that a community is intended. Zion is addressed (Isa. liv. 1-8)
as a barren woman, who has never known the pangs of child-
birth, a woman like Tamar, living in solitary dishonour. But
now this barren and lonely woman is to lift up the flaps of
her tent, and stretch them along longer cords, which will mean
that her tent-pegs must be more firmly driven in. The reason
is that her husband has returned to her and she will need to
prepare room for many children. Her old shame is removed
by this restoration of conjugal rights, and she is no longer a
virtual widow. Here too is a life-story with a happy ending;
if we did not know that the prophet is thinking of Jerusalem,
the mother-city, to which the glad news is brought across the
mountains, we might have had monographs of this unknown
female of the exile, this second Deborah who sang to the Lord
a new song, and initiated a new conquest of Canaan. It would
be worth while to print together the 'Songs of the Wife of
Yahweh' to show how far this instinct for detail can go in
the description of a whole community.

It is not necessary to multiply from other parts of the Old
Testament examples of this descriptive, though not ultimate,
individualism, especially as we encounter some of them in
dealing with the second main difficulty in the way of the
identification of Israel with the community, viz., the apparent
distinction of the Servant from the nation. This difficulty
meets us in two forms: on the one hand, the general character
of the Servant in the Songs is different from that in the rest
of Deutero-Isaiah, and, on the other, there are passages which
suggest a mission *to*, rather than *of*, Israel. These are really
important points, which deserve careful attention.

At least five impressive differences in the two portraits of the
Servant may be noted. The Servant in the Four Songs is discerning (l. 4) and obedient (l. 5); elsewhere he is described as

blind and deaf (xlii. 18 f.). On the one hand, he is represented as innocent, though he suffers for sins not his own (liii. 9, 12); on the other, he is said to be guilty, though the suffering endured for it has been excessive (xl. 2, xliii. 22, xliv. 22, xlviii. 4). The Servant of the Songs is very sure of God (xlix. 4, l. 8); elsewhere, he has lost hope in Him (xl. 27, xlix. 14). The final victory assured to the former is a victory won *through* defeat, by 'the way of the Cross' (xlii. 2-4, l. 7, liii. 7, 11 f.); but in the other case it is a victory *after* defeat (xli. 14-16, xlv. 14, xlix. 25, 26, li. 11). This victory makes the Servant, on the one hand, a world-teacher of divine truth (xlii. 1-4, xlix. 6), on the other, a world-example of divine deliverance (xliii. 10, xliv. 8), though there are points of contact. As a further point of difference, not so much of character as of fortunes, we may note that the Servant of the Songs seems to suffer as a result of his mission (l. 5, 6), whereas the Servant of the prophecies in general suffers through Babylonian rapacity and cruelty (xlii. 24, xlvii. 6).

These differences, which might be developed in further detail, form the chief argument of those who refuse to identify the two Servants. It must be admitted that the argument is impressive; in its cumulative weight, it does not depend on doubtful readings of a corrupt text, but on the salient lines of the portraits as a whole. Even those who believe that in both cases Israel is intended must find it hard to think that the *definition* of Israel, the radius of the circle drawn round 'the Servant' figure, can be the same. The blind and deaf Servant might describe the nation, from a prophetic stand-point, at any period of its history; has there ever been a nation or, indeed, a Church wholly composed of saints? But the discerning and obedient Servant could be a picture at most only of those pious and devout Israelites who were always in a minority.

The line of argument is further strengthened when we remember that there are passages in the four Songs which do suggest just such a mission of the Servant *to* the nation as would belong to men of religious passion, dwelling amongst the relatively irreligious. This is the more natural (though not the only possible) interpretation of Isa. xlix. 5, 6:

' And now 'tis the purpose of Yahweh,
  Who formed me from the womb of His Servant,
To restore Jacob to Himself,
  Gathering Israel unto Him . . .
"Too slight," He said to me, "to raise up Jacob's tribes,
And to restore the scattered of Israel; (LXX.)
So will I give thee (as) a light of nations,
That my deliverance be to earth's end."'

There is the same ambiguity in the Hebrew as in the English,
as to whether it is Yahweh or the Servant who is conceived
as restoring Jacob and gathering Israel. It must be admitted
that the suffering incurred in the third Song (l. 6) and its appeal
to God's tribunal suggest rather the experience of a Jeremiah
or a Job[2] at the hands of their fellow-countrymen, than that
of Israelite slaves or captives in the hands of foreigners. There
is a further passage in the fourth Song which in the present
text certainly distinguishes the Servant from Israel:

' For the transgression of my people was he stricken '
(liii. 8, R.V.).

It would not be safe, however, to build much on this, as the
text of this part of the Song is certainly not in its original
state. ' My people' is incongruous with the context, which
represents the kings of the nations as speaking, and the original
may have been simply ' peoples'—'Through the rebellion of
the peoples was he smitten to death' (cf. LXX.). Those who
would insist on the text as it stands, should in fairness also
insist on xlix. 3, where the Servant of the Third Song is
explicitly identified with Israel, according to the present text.

4. In view, therefore, of these considerable differences in the
two ideas of the Servant, it is not unreasonable to argue that
whilst Deutero-Isaiah is beyond question referring to the whole
of Israel in the rest of the poems, he or some other author in
the four Songs of the Servant has in view some smaller group
of higher religious quality than the mass of the nation, and
capable of being to some degree distinguished from it. But

---

[2] Cf. Duhm, *Das Buch Jesaia*, p. 284.

before we commit ourselves to this view, which would give rise to difficulties of its own, as well as to the general difficulty that such a group would hardly be of international importance, we have to ask whether the sharp antithesis between the two ideas would be as consciously felt by the thought of Israel as it is by our own, and whether there is not *some category of earlier thought which enables us to transcend it*. Such a line of thought, it is here claimed, may be found in the ancient idea of corporate personality, to which not enough attention has been paid for the interpretation of the 'Servant'.

Half a century ago, J. B. Mozley published a notable volume of lectures on the Old Testament, one of which dealt with the 'Visitation of the Sins of the Fathers upon the Children', such as the destruction of Achan's whole family as a penalty for his personal act, which he explained as a didactic accommodation to the defective sense of individual personality which marked that age. Since his time, the comparative study of religion has thrown new light upon what we might better call positively the ancient sense of corporate personality. A modern would say, with Professor McIver, 'To the primitive man the group is all. He finds himself in the group, but he never finds *himself*. He is not a personality, but one of the bearers of a type-personality. He is summed up in the group, the clan or the tribe' (*Community*, p. 332). This general principle is well illustrated from Totemism. Native tribes of Central Australia, for example, regard each individual as the direct incarnation of an Alcheringa (mythical) ancestor, whilst the totem of any man is regarded as the same thing as the man himself.[3] Thus, as Professor Lévy-Bruhl put it, 'Each individual *is* at one and the same time such and such a man, or such and such a woman, actually alive, such an ancestral individual (human or semi-human) who lived in the mythical times of the Alcheringa. and at the same time he *is* his totem, *i.e.* he participates mystically in the essence of the animal or vegetable species of which he bears the name.'[4] Since the totem represents the solidarity of the whole group, we may speak, with this writer, of a law of participation, permitting the

[3] Spencer and Gillen, *The Native Tribes of Central Australia*, p. 202.
[4] *Les Fonctions Mentales les Sociétés Inférieures*, p. 94.

tribesman to think at once of the individual in the collective and the collective in the individual, without any difficulty (*ibid.*, p. 100). So far as this is a characteristic of primitive thought (and many proofs might be given),[5] there is a fluidity of conception, a possibility of swift transition from the one to the many, and vice versa, to which our thought and language have no real parallel. When we do honour to-day to the 'Unknown Warrior', we can clearly distinguish between the particular soldier buried in the Abbey and the great multitude of whom we have consciously made him the representative. But that clearness of distinction would have been lacking to an earlier world, prior to the development of the modern sense of personality. The whole group is a unity, present in any one of its members, as Paul makes the whole race to be present in Adam. David finds it entirely natural to surrender two sons and five grandsons of Saul to the Gibeonites to expiate Saul's crime against them, and Yahweh is believed to stay the famine only when these seven men are hung up before Him. There is no consciousness here of any transition, just or unjust, from the one to the group; the point is that the group can be actually treated as one. Even when the cruder actualization of these ideas was checked by the growing recognition of the rights of the individual, the old idea is reflected in Hebrew speech, which constantly passes from the one to the many, and from the many to the one, in a way that is strange to our ears. Thus when Moses is represented as asking permission of the Edomites to pass through their land, 'Edom said unto him, Thou shalt not pass through me, lest I come out with the sword against thee. And the children of Israel said unto him, We will go up by the high way: and if we drink of thy water, I and my cattle, then will I give

[5] One of these may be found in the remark of Herodotus about Persian sacrifice (*l.c.* 132): 'For himself alone separately the man who sacrifices may not request good things in his prayer, but he prays that it may be well with all the Persians and with the king; for he himself also is included of course in the whole body of Persians' (*E.T.* by G. C. Macaulay). Another may be seen in Plato's well-known analogy between the individual and the community underlying the *Republic*, of which Webb (*Problems in the Relations of God and Man*, p. 228) says: 'It is the setting forth of a real identity of structure; the community in its structure is and must be the expression of the spiritual nature of its members.'

the price thereof' (Num. xx. 18, 19). We may also note the natural way in which 'a son of man' (Dan. vii. 13) becomes 'the saints of the most High' (vii. 27). Such a usage is much more than a conscious metaphor, as it would necessarily be for us; it echoes deep-rooted ideas of collectivity, out of which the clearer distinction of the individual and the society have but slowly emerged.[6] It explains the perplexing phenomena of many of the Psalms, in which it is still a debated question whether the individual or the community is speaking. The true answer would seem to be that it is both, or rather that there is a consciousness of both as so united in the speaker that he can emphasize now one side, now the other, without needing to draw a definite line. An example of this may be seen in the twenty-second Psalm, so closely related in its theme to the Servant of Yahweh. At one point the psalmist clearly distinguishes himself from the rest of the worshipping congregation (25); at another he speaks as a group-representative, subject to the scorn of the irreligious (6 f.); at another in terms which suggest the whole nation (12, 27 f.). The particularism of such descriptions we have already noticed; that in itself proves nothing, for the whole nation may be represented as saying, 'I am the man that hath seen affliction by the rod of his wrath' (Lam. iii. 1). But the sense of corporate personality takes us deeper than the Semitic love for individual detail, and brings us to a point of view from which it is conceivable that the prophet's mind held together what we can only regard as distinct.[7]

On this view of the Songs of the Servant we shall be able to explain the perplexing variety of interpretations offered by modern scholarship. In a sense, there is truth in each of the rival views, even the recent view of Mowinckel, that the Servant is the prophet himself. We are to think of the prophet's

---

[6] Cf. Zeph. iii. 11 : 'In that day shalt thou not be ashamed for all thy doings, wherein thou hast transgressed against me; for then I will take away out of the midst of thee thy proudly exulting ones and thou shalt no more be haughty in my holy mountain.'

[7] Cf., for example, the mediæval poems of Judah ha-Levi; 'Like the authors of the Psalms, he gladly sinks his own identity in the wider one of the people of Israel : so that it is not always easy to distinguish the personality of the speaker' (*Jewish Encyclopedia*, Vol. VII., p. 348).

consciousness as capable of a systole and diastole, an ebb and a flow, so that though he utters his own experience in the service of Yahweh, it is always with the sense implicit or explicit that these thing are true of all the devout disciples of Yahweh, and that they are Israel. We cannot, however, be true to his conception as a whole without saying that for him the Servant *is* Israel, quite apart from the question of identity of authorship with the rest of Deutero-Isaiah. Nothing less than the spectacle of Israel once humiliated, and now to be rehabilitated in the eyes of the nations of the world, will do justice to the imposing scale of the treatment in the fifty-third chapter. But when the prophet thinks of the sufferings incurred in the teaching mission of Israel, in fact if not in form he must be thinking of the experiences of those to whom religion was a reality, and the service of Yahweh, at any cost, the joy of life; probably in his deepest thoughts the prophet stood alone, like Jeremiah or Paul, and was projecting his own consciousness into that of men of lower spirituality. The sense of endowment and equipment for the prophetic office, which is exhibited in the Songs, is essentially an individual experience, though he who has it will always be moved to cry, 'Would God that all the Lord's people were prophets!' (Num. xi. 29).

5. This interpretation of the problem of the Songs of the Servant is not to be confused with that which refers it to an ideal Israel. There is truth in the remark of Bertholet, that 'the thought of an ideal Israel is so little a Semitic one, that no interpretation raises greater difficulties' (*Zu Jesaja* 53, p. 7). It is one thing to say that the prophet is always idealizing the Israel he knows, another that he is presenting us with an ideal of Israel distinct from the real Israel. In his own life, in the lives of the devout Israelites he knows, in the whole people in Babylon or elsewhere, there is a real Israel before his eyes, and of this he speaks as the Servant of Yahweh. The sufferings of this Servant are real sufferings, whether his own spiritual struggles, or the scorn endured by those who follow the prophets in faith and witness, or the agonies, physical and mental, of a nation driven into exile. The reward of the Servant will be a real and visible reward, seen in a re-peopled Jerusalem and a re-settled land and a nation honoured by

other nations. Without these actualities, it would be as difficult to conceive the Songs of the Servant as to conceive Paul's preaching of the Cross without the wooden beams and the iron nails and the torn body of the Saviour. The parallel goes deeper. Just as Paul's faith was led to transform the shame of a crucified Messiah into the glory of divine grace, so was this prophet's faith led to transform the meaning of a nation's history. The significance of his act, as we shall see, does not depend on the extent to which his ideas found currency; he might have said, with the St. Paul of F. W. H. Myers:

> 'Yea, with one voice, O world, tho' thou deniest,
> Stand thou on that side, for on this am I.'

But, as a matter of fact, we *can* trace a real succession of Israelites in whom the Songs of the Servant find their historic realization. From those disciples of Isaiah who treasured his testimony, through the men of prophetic spirit to whom we owe the Book of Deuteronomy, and that inner community of those who feared Yahweh and spoke often one to another,[8] the same community that utters its voice in the Psalter, and later on suffers martyrdom in the time of the Maccabees, right down to their true successors of the Spirit in the New Testament—not the Pharisees, but the group from whom the first disciples of Jesus were drawn—through all this long succession, in its faith, its suffering and its testimony, we can see the historic reality of the Servant of Yahweh before our eyes. When, therefore, the Christian claims the great portrait for his Lord, who stands supreme in that living succession, his claim is not so arbitrary and artificial as it has sometimes seemed when made by those who have ignored the line of history. The portrait of the Servant is, indeed, not a Messianic figure; the conception of a Messiah properly belongs to a different order and line of thought. But the two lines of Servant and Messiah are made to meet, as we shall see, in the New Testament, and they meet in Jesus of Nazareth, whose pre-eminent contribution to religious thought was to make them one.

[8] Malachi iii. 16 (about 450 B.C.).

THE SUFFERING OF THE SERVANT

NEARLY forty years ago a boy in his 'teens was whiling away the monotony of sermon-time by practising shorthand. He was much more concerned with the ideal of a verbatim record than with the rebuke of the text, 'We hid, as it were, our faces from him.' But, whilst his hand kept pace with the preacher's words to the very end, his mind and heart were taken captive by the preacher's vision of the incomparable grace of Christ, and of the ungraciousness of man's frequent attitude of indifference to Him. As the preacher reached his end, the hearer resolved to make his beginning, as a disciple of Him who is still despised and rejected of men. It was the discovery of the great evangelical appeal of suffering grace, which is the very heart of the Gospel of divine love. It is this suffering, whether in the corporate offering of the Servant of Yahweh, or in the individual Cross of Jesus of Nazareth, which is central in our study.

I. From a theological standpoint, it is the vicarious character of the suffering of the Servant which possesses supreme interest, and it should be noted that this suffering is a natural sequel of the whole character and mission of the Servant. The patient teacher of true religion described in the first Song is given a larger setting in the second, for he becomes conscious of God behind him and a world-task before him. It is the thought of the God who has equipped him for his task that enables him to put aside the temptation to feel that his work is vain, and it is God who shows him a mission that extends beyond the borders of the nation. It is in the third Song that he declares the cost of the task in suffering:

> 'I did not rebel,
> I did not turn away,

My back I gave to smiters,
My cheeks to pluckers-out (of hair)
My face I did not hide
From shameful spitting.'

Notwithstanding this suffering, his persistent purpose endures, for he is sure of God, and the fourth Song reaches the climax of the cycle, by showing that this very suffering will make possible the Servant's great achievement. The other nations had interpreted it as the penalty for Israel's sin; the vindication of Israel by its reinstatement in its own land against all expectation will bring them to a new interpretation. The suffering remains a penalty, but for the sins of the nations, not for those of Israel: ' by the stripes he bore there was healing for us.' The Servant's life, emptied out in the death of exile, though destined to be so miraculously restored, will become a sacrifice, ' a trespass-offering ', which gives the guilty nations access to Israel's God. In this world-evangelism lies the victory of the Servant, a victory yet to be won. The suffering was almost past; the vindication is yet to come. Here there are several elements that should be carefully distinguished. There is the fact of suffering, the national tragedy of the fall of Jerusalem in 586, and the exile of the nation, with all its attendant circumstances, and all the individual fortunes involved. This is the raw material, the natural sequences of history, as we should say, without any necessary religious value at all. Suffering is an evil, and it remains an evil until it is taken up into some moral transformation, that is, until a moral being reacts to it, and construes it as penalty, discipline, witness-bearing, atonement. This means that *involuntary* suffering, the experience of life's inevitabilities as such, can have no moral or religious value to the sufferer, even though it may have a moral or religious value for others, as in the vindication of law, justice, government. As such it may contribute to social education. But it becomes morally valuable to the sufferer only as he identifies himself with some moral purpose, and accepts his suffering as a just penalty, a strengthening or educative discipline, a proof of disinterested loyalty, or a means of alleviating the sufferings of others. The natural sequences that resulted in the suffering have then a changed meaning, and become part of a new and higher order. But, for the majority of Israel, this moral and religious transformation had not been wrought; their point of view was doubtless that of the current proverb, 'The fathers have eaten sour grapes, and the children's teeth are set on edge.' Their suffering remained a fact of the natural order, which awakened resentment,[1] but had no moral or religious meaning. On the other hand, the Servant, that is, the nation as represented by the prophet and all who more or less shared his outlook, transformed the meaning of the fact of suffering by their attitude towards it. So far as their sufferings were involuntary, *i.e.* those of the nation to which they belonged, this attitude meant the devout acceptance of the will of God, and the faith that it was part of His purpose for the conversion and deliverance of the world. But beyond their share in the involuntary sufferings of the nation as such, they voluntarily incurred new and greater sufferings by their mission, partly in the scorn and enmity of their own countrymen,[2] partly in that of the outside world. Such suffering was the pledge of sincerity and the manifestation of a purpose; it proved and it preached.[3] In the fourth Song, its moral and religious qualities profoundly impress the nations: 'he let himself be humbled, nor opened he his mouth.' Here, obviously, the attributes of the few are ascribed to the nation as a whole, in its corporate personality.

This corporate personality or social solidarity forms the second important feature of the Songs. We have already seen how primitive and far-reaching was the idea of corporate fellowship. Prior to the moralization of religion and of the

[1] We have evidence of this resentment being felt down into the Christian era: thus in 4 Ezra iii. it is asked why God spares the ungodly and destroys His own people: 'Have the deeds of Babylon been better than those of Zion?' (iii. 31). This should warn us against a too great or extensive idealization of Israel's attitude in the time of Deutero-Isaiah. As is fully recognized later, in regard to the sufferings of mediæval Judaism, the voluntary acceptance of suffering is necessary to give it an atoning value. But *the sufferer may be there, waiting to be transformed by the spirit of the sufferer;* part of his offering lies in the acceptance of involuntary conditions, as we see in Gethsemane.

[2] So that their suffering was part of Israel's sin, as was the Cross of Christ.

[3] Cf. *Daniel Deronda*, Ch. XLII.: 'the strongest principle of growth lies in human choice.'

idea of God, the bonds of social fellowship in Israel may be regarded as facts of the natural order, like the natural sequences of suffering. A man belonged to a family, a clan, a nation, and he necessarily suffered with it. It was only with the rise of the new individualism which we see in Jeremiah and Ezekiel that the consequences of this social solidarity came to be questioned. But with its rise there came a deepening moral consciousness, which could transform the social solidarity of the natural order and give it a moral significance, working a transformation like that in the meaning of suffering itself. We shall see this in the Maccabean martyrs, who count it a privilege, not a constraint, that they are involved in the suffering of their nation, and in an extreme degree. Their suffering is *through*, *with*, and *for* Israel. There is the same acceptance of social solidarity in the Songs, but it is not confined to Israel. The wider horizon of Deutero-Isaiah is here reflected in the faith that Israel's sufferings will avail for the whole world, and that this is Israel's supreme privilege, its means of winning the world to its God.[4] If that seems surprising in view of the intense and narrow nationalism which is found in the Old Testament, we must remember that it is by no means without parallel, so far as the universalism of outlook is concerned. By the side of the purely Jewish attitude of Nahum, exulting in the destruction of Nineveh, we must set the Catholic humanitarianism of the Book of Jonah, rejoicing in its salvation. In some of the visions of the future, Israel is content to be a third sharer with Egypt and Assyria, its ancient enemies, in the blessing of God (Isa. xix. 24, 25); Yahweh is represented as taking off the veil of the mourners and wiping the tears from the eyes of all peoples, and not of Israel alone (Isa. xxv. 7, 8); the incense and offering of many a heathen altar find acceptance with Him (Mal. i. 11). It is not, then, unexampled, except in the particular form of the idea, that Israel's endurance of suffering in the persons of its devout men should avail not for Israel only, but for all the world. Pro-

[4] Cf. Dewey and Tufts, *Ethics*, p. 102: 'The conception here reached of an interrelation which involves that the suffering of the good may be due to the sin or the suffering of others, and that the assumption of this burden marks the higher type of ethical relation, is one of the finest products of Israel's religion.'

fessor S. A. Cook seems justified in saying, 'The idea of vicarious atonement . . . was latent in the ideas of group-solidarity . . . if Israel had received double for her sins (Isa. xl. 2), might not the surplus have a saving efficacy for others? If the Servant was afflicted beyond all due, might not his extreme sufferings have a wider atoning value? Indeed, the Deutero-Isaiah is characterized by the teaching of a world-unity and a One-God; and it can fairly be urged that the idea of atonement for the group is only being extended to the utmost limits.'[5]

The third important feature in the presentaion of the Servant's suffering is the impression it makes on the nations, who declare it in the central part of the fourth Song.[6] They are moved by this spectacle of innocent, voluntary and vicarious suffering (now first seen in its true light by the vindication of Israel, its re-establishment as a people) to a confession of their sin. They were wrong in thinking these unexampled sufferings were a divine penalty; they were not a penalty, for the sufferer was innocent. But their own sins really deserved such sufferings as these. As a matter of historic fact, they see that Israel has suffered what the other nations deserved, and this substitutionary suffering has obviated the endurance of a penalty that should have been theirs:

'The chastisement bringing us welfare was on him,
And by the stripes he bore there was healing for us.'

It is important to realize that this interpretation of the suffering of Israel as penalty, the penalty due not to Israel, but to the nations, is part of a confession of sin, and is a figurative description of a restored relation to God. The Old Testament frequently uses the figure of a tribunal before which men must apear. Yahweh is pictured as having a legal controversy with the nations,[7] or with His own people,[8] which involves the forensic verdict of 'guilty' or 'innocent'. In the

---

[5] *The Cambridge Ancient History*, Vol. III., pp. 491, 492. But he inclines to the view that a real or ideal historical individual, of semi-divine character, is intended in the portrait of the Servant (*ibid.*, pp. 495, 496).
[6] Isa. liii. 1-11a: in 11b, 12, as in lii. 13-15, Yahweh is the speaker.
[7] Jer. xxv. 31.   [8] Hosea iv. 1, xii. 2.

most notable of these passages,[9] the mountains are personified as the witnesses of Israel's redemptive history, and as the court of appeal. Yahweh asks, through His prophet, why Israel has forsaken him, in view of that history; Israel, as the defendant with no reply, asks what he is to do to win favour with God, and is told of justice, mercy and humility as the divine requirements. There was a time when men gave the fruit of their body for the sin of their soul, but the prophetic religion at least had abandoned such substitution before the exile. The primary fact is the moral one, the penitent confession of sin from the nations, wrung from their lips by the sight of Israel's sufferings. Yet there is more than the ' subjective ' result. The old barbarism of a human life given physically for another here finds transformation and sublimation. Israel has suffered through the deeds of other nations. As those deeds are seen in a new light as wrongs done to Yahweh through His people, so His people's sufferings are seen in a new light as endured by them instead of the nations. The principle of substitution is indeed here, not in the cold and repellent setting of a mere transaction, but in a transformed moral relation, which robs the figure of all formality. The atmosphere is an essential part of the doctrine, and the atmosphere is the creation of moral and religious emotion, on the one hand, and of poetic imagination, the highest form of truth, on the other. Without this atmosphere, the principle of substitution becomes easily a barbarous and mechanical injustice; with it, to suffer freely for others becomes, as with the later Maccabean martyrs, the glory of a life, whether of individual or nation.[10]

[9] Micah vi. 1-8. For the procedure of the law-courts, see Deut. xxv. 1, Isa. v. 23.

[10] Cf. my statement in *The Religious Ideas of the Old Testament*, p. 147, which is somewhat misrepresented in Mr. J. K. Mozley's companion volume, *The Doctrine of the Atonement*, p. 28, through the incomplete quotation of a sentence. What I wrote was, ' Israel actually suffers as the nations should have suffered; yet the purpose of that suffering is not to satisfy divine justice, but to move the nations to penitence, and to provide the costliest of gifts with which they might approach God.' By omitting the words after ' penitence ', it is made to appear that I regard the Servant's work as ' only an object-lesson ', which I am far from doing. I think it is conceived as an atoning sacrifice; but then, as I go on to show above, this is a different thing from penalty. The over-plus of Israel's sufferings—she has received of the Lord's hand double for all her sins—is not a penalty, but a privilege, for those who share the prophet's point of view.

What, then, is the value of Israel's sufferings to God, as distinct from the influence they exert on the nations? This is the fourth point of theological importance, and its answer is to be found chiefly in the use of a technical term, *asham*, *i.e.*, 'trespass-offering':

'If ye make his life a trespass-offering,
He shall see a seed that prolongs its days.'

The trespass-offering was a form of sacrifice developed in the post-exilic Jewish religion, though having its roots in earlier religious life. A man who has withheld sacred dues from Yahweh, or committed fraud against his neighbour, must make restitution, with a fine of one-fifth added, and must further offer a ram as a trespass-offering, that the priest may make atonement for him before Yahweh.[11] The *asham* is thus a recognition of the fact that the trespass is a wrong done to Yahweh; it had to be offered to expiate a sacrilege, an invasion of God's honour, that the offender might be restored to the community.[12] The offering, like the sacrifices of the Old Testament in general, is of the nature of a gift to God; there is no suggestion in the sacrifices of the Old Testament that any *penalty* rests on the victim. We may speak of substitution so far as we use the different figure of a tribunal; but sacrifice proper has nothing to do with a tribunal, nor did it, in the Old Testament, imply substitution. But sacrifice can be, amongst other things, the means of restoring a broken relation, according to ancient ideas of the relation of God and man. It is natural to approach an offended superior with a placatory gift, and with this instinct man offered sacrifices to God. The sufferings of Israel as the Servant of Yahweh are not, literally, a sacrifice, but they may be figuratively described as an offering through which the nations who have offended God may now draw near to Him in their penitence. Israel achieves something through its loyal service which is acceptable to

[11] Lev. v. 14 to vi. 7.
[12] Driver, *Encyclopædia of Religion and Ethics*, Vol. V., p. 658; Dussaud, *Les Origines Cananéennes du Sacrifice Israélite*, p. 127; Buchanan Gray, *Sacrifice in the Old Testament*, pp. 57 f.

God; the nations who ally themselves with Israel's religion stand to gain whatever favour that service wins, and Israel's seed is thus prolonged in them, when they make Israel's offered life their trespass-offering.

When, therefore, we ask what the prophet meant by the words, 'My servant shall justify many,' we must not try to read into them later systems of atonement, Rabbinical or Christian. The prophet's desire is to interpret the mystery of Israel's suffering, which goes so far beyond her moral deserts. The interpretative principle he applies is the conception of Israel's mission to the world, as the prophet and missionary of true religion. This prophetic mission involves suffering, in addition to the suffering Israel has incurred as a nation. But the suffering is not meaningless or fruitless. When it is past, and Israel is restored to her place, the world will see the suffering to be vicarious. It can be described at once both as the penalty which belonged to the nations and as the sacrifice through which the nations may approach God. From the prophet's standpoint, that is a sufficient answer. The author of Job taught (in the Prologue) that the suffering of the innocent could be a proof of disinterested service, and (in the Epilogue) that Job could be an intercessor for his faulty friends. The author of the Songs said that disinterested service involving suffering could both touch the hearts of men by its generosity, and form a way of access for others to God by its sacrificial character. But neither the Servant nor Job is conceived to be actually enduring a penalty; both the world of the Servant and the friends of Job thought that, and they were both wrong. If we could ask the prophet just how this sacrificial service of suffering made a difference, he might have said, could he have spoken our language, that that fact of Israel's suffering had enriched the world with new moral and spiritual values, precious to God, and that the extension of Israel's corporate personality to a larger Israel made those values available for every one who hungered and thirsted after righteousness.

2. It will have been noticed that nothing has so far been said of any relation of the Songs to the Old Testament figure of the Messiah, with which they come to be so closely united

in the New Testament. Indeed, the identification of the Servant with Jesus of Nazareth in Christian thought has made it difficult for the Christian student of the Songs to consider them apart from Him. Surprise is often expressed that the Cross of the Messiah should have been a stumbling-block to the Jew when Isaiah liii. gives it so emphatic and striking a place. Yet this surprise springs from a double misunderstanding—first, the impression that an individual person was clearly designated by the Songs from the outset, and second, that this person was not less clearly identified with the expected Messiah. We have seen the strong grounds for holding that the Servant in the Songs is Israel as a nation, though its mission and fortunes are expressed in terms appropriate only to certain groups or individuals within the nation. The suffering of Israel is indeed the most prominent feature of the portrait, but the sporadic suffering of a larger or smaller group in successive generations could not arrest the attention like the sufferings of a single supreme individual. Further, Jesus of Nazareth was supreme for Christian faith in the first generation because He was believed to be the Messiah, and therefore a unique significance belonged to all that befell Him. But the portrait of the Servant in the Songs has no direct relation to the Messianic hope of Israel. That hope was primarily in the restoration of a glorified and exalted Davidic kingship, of a strongly marked political character. The development of Israel's religion gave a moral and religious content to this hope, as one to be fulfilled in just and peaceful government, inward uprightness matched by outward prosperity. In these anticipations of the future, the figure and function of the ' Anointed ' representative of God are much less prominent than we might have expected, and are often wanting altogether. Even where he appears, and in his most pacific form (e.g. Zech. ix. 9 f.), he offers nothing comparable with the suffering of the Servant, and the chief resemblance is in the fact that both the Servant and the Messiah, by their very different paths, are brought to a final victory. This real difference agrees with the fact that there was no conception of a suffering Messiah in the Judaism of the New Testament times. The Messiah who dies after a life of four hundred years, according to one Pseudepigraphical book

(4 Ezra vii. 28, 29), is no true parallel, and the later Talmudic reference to the Messiah ben Joseph who is slain (Sukkah 52b) is of no more real account. So far as the later Judaism connected the idea of suffering with the Messiah, the reason for such Rabbinical conceptions may probably be found in the actual sufferings of the time of Bar Cochba's revolt in the second century A.D.[13] It is also significant that whilst the Targum of Jonathan—a free Aramaic paraphrase of the third or fourth Christian century—identifies the Servant with the Messiah, the references to his suffering are transferred to the people, Israel, so that we read, for example, instead of 'we reckoned him smitten, stricken of God and afflicted', 'we were reckoned to be smitten, stricken of God and afflicted.'

Jewish exegesis, both in mediæval and modern times, has for the most part regarded the suffering Servant as Israel,[14] and with ample justification from the actual course of the national history. As an example of the mediæval exegete we may take Rashi, of the eleventh century, who represents the nations as saying, 'Israel suffered in order that by his sufferings atonement might be made for all other nations; the sickness which ought to have fallen upon us was carried by him.'[15] As an example of the modern Jewish interpretation we may take Dr. Kohler: 'Whatever be the historical background of this great elegy, our seer uses it to portray Israel as the tragic hero

[13] The opinion of a competent Jewish scholar is worth quoting: 'Such ideas as we find elsewhere (e.g. Messiah ben Joseph, the suffering Messiah, etc.) are popular accretions dating after the Destruction of the Temple and the fall of Bittir, when the sore afflictions and the defeat of Bar Kokhbah served to provide the colouring for the lurid descriptions or visions of vengeance, together with the vivid and multicoloured pictures of redemption' (J. Klausner, *Jesus of Nazareth*, p. 201). Cf. Bousset, *Kyrios Christos*[2], p. 25; Stanton in Hastings' *Dictionary of the Bible*, Vol. III, pp. 354, 355; Buttenwieser in *Jewish Encyclopedia*, Vol. VIII., pp. 505 f.; J. Weiss, *Das Urchristentum*, p. 80.

[14] The earliest reference to Isaiah liii. is in Daniel xii. 3, where the Hebrew of 'they that turn many to righteousness' echoes Isaiah liii. 11, 'he shall make many righteous'. This implies a collective interpretation of the Servant, as also does the parallel passage in Wisdom ii. 12 f., partly quoted on p. 58.

[15] *The Fifty-Third Chapter of Isaiah, according to the Jewish Interpreters*, by Driver and Neubauer, Vol. II., p. 38. They cite the Midrash Rabbah on Deut. xxiii., 'the Israelites poured out their soul to die in the captivity, as it is said, "Because he poured out his soul to die".'

of the world's history . . . seeing Israel as a man of woe and grief, chosen by Providence to undergo unheard-of trials for a great cause, by which, at the last, he is to be exalted. Bent and disfigured by his burden of misery and shame, shunned and abhorred as one laden with sin, he suffers for no guilt of his own. He is called to testify to his God among all the peoples, and is thus the *Servant of the Lord*, the atoning sacrifice for the sins of mankind, from whose bruises healing is to come to all the nations.'[16]

No doubt Jewish exegesis has been unconsciously influenced by its environment and interests towards a collective interpretation, as Christian exegesis until recent times towards an individualistic interpretation. But for those very reasons it is valuable for the Christian theologian to study the songs in the light of the history of the Jewish nation. This may not only deliver him from some of his own tendencies, but also confirm the interpretation we have reached on purely exegetical grounds. In any case, our theological concern is with the conception of suffering which the Songs present, and this is largely independent of the identification of the Sufferer. The link with the New Testament for modern exegesis is not to be found in the anticipation of an individual sufferer so much as in the reality of the suffering, the attitude towards it, and the interpretation of its mystery. The true preparation made in the Old Testament for the New lies in the continuity of truth, not in the superficial resemblance of its particular manifestations. If the Songs of the Servant, originally spoken of the nation Israel, are found to involve great truths about suffering which are also exhibited historically in Jesus of Nazareth, then we have a surer ground of appeal to the 'argument from prophecy' than in such external resemblances as the association of Joseph of Arimathæa with the words 'with the rich in his death', which themselves are probably due to a textual error.

George Eliot, in the novel, *Daniel Deronda*, a memorable presentation of Jewish aspirations, has quoted some sentences of Leopold Zunz which have become classical. 'If there are ranks in suffering, Israel takes precedence of all the nations—

[16] *Jewish Theology*, pp. 371, 372.

if the duration of sorrows and the patience with which they are borne ennoble, the Jews are among the aristocracy of every land—if a literature is called rich in the possession of a few classic tragedies, what shall we say to a National Tragedy lasting for fifteen hundred years, in which the poets and the actors were also the heroes?' In the context of that quotation, George Eliot shows that she is fully aware of the protest it is apt to raise—that the successful materialism of the Jew is even more in evidence than his tragic spirituality. 'This Jeshurun of a pawnbroker,' she writes of one of her characters, 'was not a symbol of the great Jewish tragedy; and yet was there not something typical in the fact that a life like Mordecai's—a frail incorporation of the national consciousness, breathing with difficult breath—was nested in the self-gratulating ignorant prosperity of the Cohens?'[17]

One of the most impressive catalogues of the sufferings of Israel on the visible and physical side is to be found in the chapter of Zunz's book[18] which is introduced by the words already quoted. Its fifty pages contain a startling record from the time of the Crusades onwards. The mobs which accompanied or were aroused by the Crusaders found a congenial and convenient Crusade of their own in the massacre of Jews, as notably in the Rhine valley, where four thousand are said to have been done to death in the first Crusade. 'When the crusaders at last stormed Jerusalem, July 15, 1099, they drove all the Jews into one of the synagogues, and there burned them alive.'[19] The Jews were always liable to calumny, such as the charge of poisoning wells in time of plague, and Zunz says that the epidemic of the fourteenth century known as the Black Death brought them worse consequences than even the Crusades.[20] The torture and burning of Jews under the Inquisition, especially in Spain, are well known; their expulsion from that country in 1492 had its parallels in their expulsion from England two centuries, and from France, one century, earlier. There followed 'that black age in Jewish life, the

---

[17] *Daniel Deronda*, Ch. XLII., second paragraph.
[18] *Die synagogale Poesie des Mittelalters*, p. 9-58.
[19] *Jewish Encyclopedia*, Vol. IV., p. 379.
[20] *Op. cit.*, p. 39.

sixteenth century, the century of the Ghetto and degradation.'[21] Before these mediæval times there are centuries of repressive legislation, from the time that the Jew was forbidden to enter Jerusalem, on the suppression of Bar Cochba's revolt. Our own times have known the meaning of Anti-Semitism, notably in the pogromy of Russia.[22] We are not here concerned with the causes of the unpopularity of the Jews in ancient or modern times, as for example the national exclusiveness which Tacitus stigmatized.[23] The point which does concern us in regard to the suffering of the Servant of Yahweh is that Israel as a nation has suffered uniquely. The actuality of the suffering, to which the Songs point, has received abundant illustration in the later history.

What has been the attitude of the finest spirits of Israel towards the fact of this unexampled suffering? We cannot answer this question better than by turning to the greatest religious poet of Judaism in the Middle Ages, Judah ha-Levi (1085-1140), and to his famous 'Ode to Zion', which legend represents him as chanting when he came into sight of his long-desired Jerusalem, only to be slain by the lance of a passing Arab.[24] It was he who said that 'Israel is amongst the nations as the heart among the limbs',[25] and the 'Ode' is written in that key.[26]

'Sadly he greets thee still,
    The prisoner of hope, who, day and night,
Sheds ceaseless tears, like dew on Hermon's hill.
Would that they fell upon thy mountain's height! . . .
Thy air is life unto my soul, thy grains
Of dust are myrrh, thy streams with honey flow:
Naked and barefoot, to thy ruined fanes
How gladly would I go: . . .

[21] Israel Abrahams, *Jewish Life in the Middle Ages*, p. 64.
[22] *Encyclopædia of Religion and Ethics*, Vol. I., p. 596.
[23] *Histories*, Bk. V., ch. 5: 'adversus omnes alios hostile odium.'
[24] Joseph Jacobs, *Jewish Ideals*, pp. 103-131, 'Jehuda Halevi, Poet and Pilgrim.'
[25] *Ibid.*, p. 127.
[26] The translation quoted is that by Alice Lucas, in *The Jewish Year*, pp. 90 f.

To what can be compared the majesty
Of thy anointed line?
To what the singers, seers, and Levites thine?
The rule of idols fails and is cast down;
Thy power eternal is, from age to age thy crown.'

In this passionate devotion to Zion and Zion's God, the sufferings of Israel become for Israel's poets a priestly offering; a poem of Jacob ben Judah which commemorates a martyr of the thirteenth century represents him as saying, ' I am a priest, about to offer my body to my God.'[27] This is the theme of the prophet of the Songs of the Servant of Yahweh, the thought expressed by Bourget when he says, ' Nothing is lost when we make an offering of it.' But there is no more impressive example of this attitude than that of the interpreters of the Maccabean martyrdoms. The first Jewish answer to the persecution of Antiochus Epiphanes in the second century before Christ was not the armed revolt of Mattathias and his heroic sons, but the passive endurance of suffering by such men as the aged Eleazar and the seven brethren.[28] They are represented as consciously accepting the sufferings unjustly inflicted by their persecutors as a just recompense for the sins of Israel, and as they hope, the final instalment of that recompense due to God: ' We are suffering for our own sins, and though our living Lord is angry for a little, in order to rebuke and chasten

---

[27] Quoted by Reinach, *Histoire des Israélites*, p. 152. We may compare the remark of Philo, *De Abrah.*, Vol. II., p. 15 (quoted by Box, in *The Journal of Theological Studies*, April 1912, p. 325): ' Israel is above all the nations beloved of God, one that has received the priesthood for the whole human race.' Professor Box asks (*ibid.*, p. 329), ' how can the sufferings of the Jewish race in exile be said to be vicarious? ' My answer would be on the lines of Bourget's saying, quoted above. Suffering is the raw material, without any moral or religious value till it is shaped by a moral or religious attitude. Not many Jews, perhaps, have transformed their national sufferings into a sacrifice. But then, how many within Christianity have failed to learn the lesson of the Cross? Wherever there is kinship of spirit with the Sufferer on that Cross, Christian, Jewish or ethnic, we must believe there is an acceptable offering to God. But it would be difficult to show that Judaism has kept the sense of a mission to the Gentiles in the spirit of Deutero-Isaiah, and it would be far too much to expect in mediæval times. For a good account of this spirit in Jewish thought see the introduction to R. Levy's *Deutero-Isaiah* (1925).

[28] 1 Macc. i. 61 f.; 2 Macc. vi. and vii.

us, he will again be reconciled to his own servants. . . . I, like my brothers, give up body and soul for our fathers' laws, calling on God to show favour to our nation soon . . . and to let the Almighty's wrath, justly fallen on the whole of our nation, end in me and in my brothers.'[29] Here we have an instructive example of the manner in which a ' fact ' of experience is transformed in meaning by a different attitude towards it. The suffering of the martyrs is at one and the same time a sin on the part of their persecutors, and a just sentence on the part of God on the sins of Israel. The martyrs do not complain that they, being personally innocent, are involved in the sufferings of guilty Israel; they accept Israel's corporate personality as involving themselves, and glory in the opportunity for this service to their brethren. This attitude becomes more clearly articulate in the homiletical treatment of the martyrdoms which forms the so-called Fourth Book of Maccabees :

' Be gracious to thy people, being satisfied with our penalty on their behalf. Make my blood their purification, and take my life as the substitute for theirs.'

' Because of them the enemy had no more power over our people, and the tyrant was punished, and the fatherland purified, inasmuch as they have become a substitute for (the life forfeited by) the sin of the people; and through the blood of those pious men and their propitiatory death, the divine Providence rescued Israel that before was afflicted.'[30]

Here there is a mingling of several lines of thought, which ought to be clearly disentangled. There is (1) the bare fact of physical suffering, (2) the unjust infliction of this suffering by the persecutors, (3) the admission that suffering is justly due

[29] 2 Macc. vii. 33, 37, 38. In the *Assumption of Moses*, ix. 7, where Eleazar is made to say, ' if we do this and die, our blood shall be avenged before the Lord,' the thought is somewhat different; God will be compelled to do something by the suffering of the innocent. The idea of substitution is found in the *Testament* of Benjamin iii. 8, though this may be an interpolation.

[30] 4 Macc. vi. 28, 29; xvii. 21, 22. The Hellenistic character of this book must not be forgotten; cf. J. Weiss, *Das Urchristentum*, p. 84.

for the sins of Israel, (4) the endurance of the suffering by those who are not guilty of such sins, (5) the interpretation of the suffering in the legal terms of a penalty, (6) the interpretation of the suffering in sacrificial terms as purificatory and propi- tiatory, (7) the principle of substitution by which one life is to be allowed to replace another. This last, which is the crucial point, comes into operation because the sufferers themselves belong to Israel; it is assumed that any contribution they make personally falls to the common stock of Israel. Indeed, the very term 'substitution' is misleading in this connection; it suggests an arbitrary and external transaction, whereas the prayer of the martyrs springs from the racial bond, as some- thing natural and instinctive. In one sense, this, of course, takes something away from the sacrificial aspect of their deaths, as Koeberle points out: 'If they suffer for the people, it is because they too are Jews. There is wanting the most important element, viz. that the pious man voluntarily takes the sin of others into his consciousness, and experiences it as his own through love—that he becomes one with the guilty on moral lines, and not on the ground of physical association.'[31] That difference should be remembered when we come to con- sider the vicarious suffering of the Cross of Christ. We have also to remember that the vicarious interpretation of the suffering of the Maccabean martyrs is only one element, and relatively a small one, in the whole representation of their glorious testimony.[32] But it remains one of the most notable links between the Songs of the Servant and the New Testament interpretation of them, and it is not surprising that one exegete (Bertholet) should have proposed to take the chief part of the fifty-third of Isaiah as an ode in honour of Eleazar the martyr. Certainly, there could be found no closer parallel from Jewish literature and history, so far as the general interpretation of suffering goes. There was clearly a Pharisaic 'Quietism'[33]

---

[31] *Sünde und Gnade*, p. 594. Koeberle gives the best analysis of the signi- ficance of these martyrdoms which I have seen.

[32] Cf. Deissmann, *ad. loc.*, 'the whole idea arose not as a stereotyped dogmatic proposition, but through the secret and daring intuition of religious feeling' (Kantzsch's *Pseudepigraphen*, p. 160).

[33] Charles, in *Apocrypha and Pseudepigrapha*, Vol. II., p. 407; cf. Andrews, in *Mansfield College Essays*, p. 84.

which valued the martyrdoms of the Maccabean age more highly that its militant heroes, and so far might be held to have prepared for the doctrine of a suffering Messiah.

The development of religion in the three centuries between the Servant and the Maccabean martyrs has led to one important difference which should be noted, and is confirmation of the collective as against the individualistic view of the Songs. These martyrs are represented as looking for a continuance of individual life beyond death, though this is conceived in 2 Maccabees as a resurrection of the body, and in 4 Maccabees as an immortality of the soul. This is in accordance with the eschatology which developed subsequently to the exile, and is first found in an apocalypse now included in the Book of Isaiah (xxvi. 19), and then in the Book of Daniel (xii. 2), of Maccabean times. We have no doctrine of individual resurrection in any writing of pre-exilic or exilic times. The impressive vision of the Valley of Dry Bones (Ezek. xxxvii.) is of the resurrection of a *nation* to a new corporate life, out of the grave of exile. Now the fifty-third of Isaiah definitely describes the death and burial of the Servant, followed by a divine deliverance and vindication, which must imply a resurrection of some kind.[34] If, as we have been led to think, this means a national resurrection, a re-establishment of Israel in its own land, we have an exact parallel with the contemporary vision of the Valley of Dry Bones. But if it meant the resurrection of an individual person—and how else could he be vindicated after his death and burial?—then we should have no parallel for centuries. It would therefore seem that the collective conception of suffering with a vicarious interpretation is matched by the conception of a collective ' resurrection '—both ideas being much more easily reached along the lines of social solidarity than of individual destiny and therefore attained at a much earlier date. As the idea of individualism develops, it is applied both to the idea of vicarious suffering and to that of ' resurrection '.

[34] Thus, according to Duhm, it is a definite prophecy of the resurrection of an individual man of God, who has died of leprosy.

III

THE MESSIAH-SERVANT

OUR previous study of the Servant of Yahweh has led us to two principal conclusions, viz., that the Servant is primarily the nation Israel in its world-mission of making known the religion of Yahweh, and that the actual pursuit of this mission by the true servants of Yahweh within the nation involved suffering, with a vicarious and sacrificial value for the world's forgiveness. It is important to realize the actuality of this suffering and its inevitableness in an irreligious and sinful world, because the recognition of this removes one of the chief prejudices against any form of vicarious atonement. The Songs of the Servant are an explanation of the mystery of a suffering already realized, not a doctrinal speculation out of touch with actual life. The sufferings of devout men for their religious faith and mission will be differently explained by those who share and by those who reject that faith; but the sufferings are there to be explained, and are not artificially imposed.[1] We have outlined their continuity through the centuries between the Exile and the present day, so far as Judaism is concerned. We have now to examine that special appropriation of the conception of the Servant which is made in the New Testament Gospel. Here, also, we shall find that the suffering of Jesus was a mystery that called for explanation, an actuality that was there before there could be any speculation as to its meaning or necessity. From one point of view, the Cross would seem inevitable, if not deserved; from another, it was ultimately seen as a voluntary sacrifice, with far-reaching meaning. In this process of interpretation, within and without the consciousness of Jesus Himself, the figure of the Servant of Yahweh exercised a most notable influence.

[1] Cf. the remark in the second chapter (p. 82) that the moral and spiritual value of the suffering must lie in the attitude of the sufferer to it.

1. There is a sentence in one of the Songs of the Servant in which he describes himself as a smooth arrow from God's quiver (xlix. 2). If we appropriate this sentence to Jesus, and develop its imagery, we may say that the shaft of the arrow was His consciousness of sonship, its barb the conviction that sprang from sonship that He was the promised Messiah, and its feathers the guiding conception of His mission drawn from the Servant of Yahweh. It is generally recognized by New Testament exegetes that ' It is the filial, not the messianic consciousness of Jesus which is the basis of Christianity '.[2] We can bring practically all His teaching and activity under the category of a divine sonship, and its extension into the sonship which He sought to elicit or create in other hearts. Here we may venture to believe, was the content of His own inner life, as well as of His expression of that inner life in word and deed. Sonship is the most adequate and permanent of the New Testament concepts of the Person of Christ, because the most universal. Jesus took this human analogy to deepen and enrich it by a new moral and religious realization of its possibilities, which remains true to the concept itself. On the other hand, though the Jewish conception of a ' Messiah' is of great importance for primitive Christianity, its significance speedily became historical only. ' Jesus is the Christ was soon replaced by ' Jesus is Lord' outside Jewish Christianity. Not only so, but Jesus Himself so profoundly modified the Messianic conception, so far as He adopted it, that we may easily be misled in speaking of Him as the Messiah at all. For the Davidic or political form of the conception He had little or no use, whilst the transcendental Messiah of Jewish apocalyptic participates in that ethical and religious transformation which apocalyptic in general received at His hands. We have one of the chief guiding principles of that transformation in the conception of the Servant, which Jesus for the first time blended with that of the Messiah.[3]

Definite evidence of this connection meets us on the very threshold of the public ministry of Jesus, in the experience

---

[2] Moffatt, The Theology of the Gospels, p. 132. See, also, the careful and illuminating discussion in Dominus Noster, by C. A. Anderson Scott (pp. 151 f.).   [3] Moffatt, The Theology of the Gospels, p. 149.

of His baptism.   According to the simplest narrative of it,
that of Mark (i. 9-11), His vision of the open heavens and of
the descending Spirit was accompanied by a voice which said,
'Thou art my beloved Son, in thee I am well pleased.'   This
sentence combines two Old Testament quotations, taken res-
pectively from the second Psalm, 'Thou art my Son,' and
from the first of the Servant Songs (xlii. 1), 'in whom my soul
delighteth.'[4]   So far as the saying faithfully reflects the consciousness of Jesus, it warrants us in the belief that His baptism
marks 'the hour in which a new conception of the Messiah
was born.'[5]   No doubt, other Messianic passages also had been
assimilated by His consciousness, through that long study of
the Old Testament Scriptures which His subsequent teaching
reveals.   The reference to the descent of the Spirit suggests
the endowment of the Messiah according to Isaiah xi. 2 f., 'the
Spirit of Yahweh shall rest upon him'; we recall the direct
application to Himself of Isaiah lxi. 1, 'The Spirit of the Lord
God is upon me,' made in the synagogue at Nazareth.[6]   But
our impression that the reference to the Servant is primary
is confirmed by the sequel to the baptism, viz., the Temptation.
Just as this involved the newly found Messianic consciousness
—'if thou art the Son of God',[7] so it involved a new conception of the meaning of that Messiahship, in harmony with the
moral and religious character of the Servant, not with a
political kingship.

The evidence, however, becomes more impressive when we
think of that other baptism which awaited Jesus—the baptism
of His death.[8]   If the distinctive feature in the portrait of the
Servant was his suffering, so the distinctive feature in the
portrait of Jesus in the Gospels is His Cross and Passion.   The
shadow of that Cross fell over His path long before He reached
it, and was accepted by Him as part of the inscrutable will of
God.   But where did He gain His confidence that this was the

---

[4] The same verb in the version of Theodotion : ὃν ηὐδόκησεν ἡ ψυχή
μου.
[5] Feine, *Theologie des Neuen Testaments*,³ p. 66.
[6] Luke iv. 18 f.; a passage similar to the Songs of the Servant, though
not belonging to the original cycle.   Cf. the significant reference to this
passage in the message to John the Baptist, Matt. xi. 5.
[7] Matt. iv. 3; Luke iv. 3.   [8] Mark x. 38, 39; Luke xii. 50.

will of God, so as to declare it beforehand to his disciples,[9] if not from the suffering of the Servant?[10] 'The Son of man goeth, even as it is written of Him.'[11] Even if some of the references of this kind are due to the later attestation of the Gospel story from the Old Testament by the interpretative faith of the early Christians, yet we have still to account for the acceptance of death by Jesus as part of the Messianic mission, and there is no explanation so simple and direct, as that He was profoundly influenced by 'the Servant of Yahweh' before and in and after the baptismal hour. Here, in Isaiah liii., there was the one indubitable and sufficient basis for the faith of the disciples that Christ died for our sins 'according to the Scriptures', when once the application to the Messiah was made; but that which explains the faith of the disciples might with equal justice be used to explain the shaping of the conviction in the mind of their Master. This general line of argument gives a new force to indications of the influence of the Servant passages upon the consciousness of Jesus which we might hesitate to press if they stood alone. Chief among these are the reference to His death as a 'ransom' and as a 'covenant'. Jesus was defining true greatness in the Kingdom as unselfish and sacrificial service, when He declared that even He came to give His life like a ransom *for many*.[12] Similarly in the Upper Room, according to the Marcan tradition, Jesus identifies the cup with the blood of the covenant shed *for many*.[13] The peculiar nature of this repeated phrase in such solemn context is best explained as a conscious reference to Isaiah liii. 11, 12: 'my servant shall justify many'; 'he bare the sin of many,' especially when we remember the emphasis on service in the earlier New Testament context, and on the voluntary giving of life in both passages.[14] It is true that neither the

[9] Mark viii. 31; ix. 31; x. 34.
[10] The only parallel would be Ps. xxii., actually quoted on the Cross, and this is much less direct.
[11] Mark xiv. 21.   [12] Mark x. 45.   [13] Mark xiv. 24.
[14] So Feine, *op cit.*, p. 84; Weiss, *Das Urchristentum*, p. 84; Rashdall, *The Idea of Atonement in Christian Theology*, p. 32; Moffatt, *op. cit.*, p. 145; Cave, *The Doctrine of the Person of Christ*, p. 27, note ' The otherwise mysterious reference to the " many " is almost certainly to be explained by the corresponding phrases of Isa. liii., " He shall bear the sins of many "; " He shall justify many ".'

word 'ransom' nor the word 'covenant' occurs in the Servant Songs (though 'covenant' occurs in the immediate context of two of them, viz., xlii. 6, xlix. 8 : 'I give thee for a covenant of people' and the verb corresponding to 'ransom' occurs in Isa. lii. 3 : 'ye shall be ransomed without money'); but exegetical emphasis ought not to fall on the precise figure employed by Jesus, so much as on the general intention of His words. In reference to the ransom, Schlatter[15] rightly says that the word brings all the thoughts of Christ which are concerned with the Cross under the general rule of obedience. He did not ask or explain why a ransom should be necessary, why God should demand it. He gives His life to God, and God gives the new community to Him. He does not look beyond the necessity springing from the will of God, that His mission involves death, and this He humbly yet proudly accepts. All this is fully in line with the fifty-third of Isaiah, and could have been learnt as well from no other passage of Scripture. The Servant also, as represented by the prophet, faces the unexplained mystery of suffering and brings it into line with his mission, thus coming to accept it as the will of God. In neither instance must we look for any explanation of the necessity of a trespass-offering or of a ransom or of a covenant-sacrifice. These are themselves held to be sufficient explanations of that which is in the nature of things as God has willed them. The emphasis falls on the attitude of the sufferer, not on the precise nature or amount of the suffering.

It would be easy to point out many other lines of possible influence, when the essential contact has once been proved, such as the extension of the mission of the Servant from Israel to the world (cf. Luke i. 32, Matt. xxii. 8, 9), or the silence of the Servant under suffering (John xix. 9). But there is no need to turn to general principles which might have been gathered elsewhere, or to particular parallels which may possibly be due to the New Testament writers (Mark iv. 12, Luke xxii. 37), and are often superficial (e.g. Matt. viii. 17, xii. 17 f.). Quite apart from these, the evidence of crucial moments in the Lord's life and of His explicit attitude to His own approaching death warrants us in saying with Moffatt :

[15] *Die Geschichte des Christus*, pp. 428-36.

' that the suffering Servant conception was organic to the consciousness of Jesus, and that He often regarded His vocation in the light of this supremely suggestive prophecy.'[16]

2. When we turn from the study of the consciousness of Jesus to that of His disciples, the evidence of the influence of the Servant-passages is much more copious and direct, though not really more impressive and convincing. They must lie behind the words of the stranger on the way to Emmaus, though not forming the whole of the reference there: ' Behoved it not the Christ to suffer these things, and to enter into his glory? '[17] In the preaching of the early Church, as recorded in the Acts, the conception of the ' Servant ' becomes one of the chief categories under which the Person of Christ is presented. ' The God of our fathers hath glorified His Servant Jesus '; ' God, having raised up His Servant, sent him to bless you, in turning away every one of you from your iniquities '; ' Thy holy Servant Jesus, whom thou didst anoint '; ' the name of thy holy Servant Jesus.'[18] The story of the Ethiopian eunuch who was engrossed in the perplexing study of the fifty-third of Isaiah when Philip encountered him, is, no doubt, a typical one.[19] The First Epistle of Peter gives a central place to the quotation of Isaiah liii. 5, 6, 9 to illustrate the patience of Christ: ' who did no sin, neither was guile found in his mouth: who, when he was reviled, reviled not again; when he suffered, threatened not; but committed himself to him that judgeth righteously: who his own self bare our sins in his body upon the tree, that we, having died unto sins, might live unto righteousness; by whose stripes ye were healed. For ye were going astray like sheep; but are now returned unto the Shepherd and Bishop of your souls.'[20] The passage shows how aptly the description of the Servant could be applied to Jesus, and also how fully and freely such dominating passages might be reproduced without any formal citation, so that we should not know that it was a quotation, if the original were not before us. This free use of Isaiah liii. is to be found in a passage of great theological importance, where its influence

---

[16] *Op. cit.,* p. 149.
[17] Luke xxiv. 26, cf. ver. 46.
[18] Acts iii. 13, 26; iv. 27, 30.

[19] Acts viii., 27-39.
[20] Peter ii. 22-25.

has not been adequately recognized, viz., Philippians ii. Here also the example of Christ is urged, but Paul characteristically contrasts the humiliation of the Cross with the pre-existent rank of Christ, which He voluntarily abandoned to win the new name of 'Lord'.[21] His exaltation is described in terms obviously drawn from Isaiah xlv. 23: 'that in the name of Jesus every knee should bow, and every tongue confess that Jesus Christ is Lord.' But it may well be that the Songs of the Servant, belonging to the general context of this direct quotation, have subtly but deeply shaped the Apostle's thought here.[22] 'God highly exalted him' echoes the opening words of the fourth Song, 'my Servant shall be high and greatly exalted,' just as 'he humbled himself' echoes the Greek version of liii. 8 (as quoted in Acts viii. 33), 'in his humiliation'. In both passages a remarkable humiliation is followed by a not less remarkable vindication and glory, and in both the central figure is a Servant ('taking the form of a Servant,' Phil. ii. 7). But the most remarkable parallel is one that has not apparently been recognized, because it does not lie on the surface. Paul has used a very peculiar phrase to express the voluntary acceptance of humiliation by Christ, viz., 'he emptied himself,' and then, after three participial clauses ('taking the form of a Servant', 'being made in the likeness of men', 'being found in fashion as a man') the phrase is either paralleled or continued in a more familiar one, 'he humbled himself, becoming obedient to death.'[23] In the Hebrew text

---

[21] The idea of a descent of the 'Heavenly Man' is found in contemporary thought (e.g., Poimandres, as quoted by Moffatt, *Introduction to the Literature of the New Testament*, p. 172) and Paul may have been influenced by this.

[22] So Bindley, *Expositor*, Dec. 1923 (p. 443): 'The Old Testament passage which seems to have informed and coloured St. Paul's language and thought throughout these verses is Isaiah liii. 12.'

[23] It may be objected that these clauses, referring to the Incarnation, ought to be taken as defining the scope of the previous verb, 'He emptied himself,' just as 'becoming obedient unto death' defines the scope of the verb in the words 'He humbled himself'. To insist on this, when there are reasons to the contrary, seems to force the Apostle's language into too rigorous a mould; the dictation of his letters, and the fertility of his mind, often led to the introduction of parenthetical clauses. Thus in Romans ii. 13 f., the thought of future justification (13) at The Day of Judgment (16) is interrupted by a reference (14, 15) to the present testimony of the heathen

of Isaiah liii. 12, we find the very phrases Paul here used, 'He emptied himself to death,' and 'he let himself be humbled.' This would suggest that Paul was not thinking primarily of the Incarnation, but of the Crucifixion, which is much more characteristic of his general thought,[24] and that the participial clauses which refer to the human life were inserted (in the Apostle's parenthetic way) to bridge the gap between the pre-existent state of glory and the humiliation of the Cross. Jesus, in fact, became the Servant of God on earth in order to empty out Himself to death, and the Kenosis was properly that of the Crucifixion, though naturally involving the Incarnation.[25]

3. The New Testament application of the Songs of the Servant was to the individual life and work of Jesus the Messiah, in whom they found so apt a fulfilment. But the very fact that Judaism, as we have seen, could maintain, later on if not then, the original reference of the Songs to Israel collectively, may remind us that the 'individualism' of the ancient world was much more expansive than we are apt to think. We have only to remember the important place taken by the doctrine of corporate personality in the teaching of the Apostle Paul

conscience. So here, where Paul's dominant thought is as usual the death of Christ on the Cross, which he is contrasting with that 'equality with God' which was accessible to His heavenly being. But when he has begun to express this divine humiliation unto death, with the memorable words of Isa. liii. 12 in his mind as its apt expression, he checks himself after saying, 'He emptied himself——' before adding the completing words 'to death,' at the remembrance of the human life which was the necessary pathway to that death of the Cross, and describes the humiliation of this life on earth as a 'servant' prior to the great humiliation of the Cross; hence the parenthetical clauses, which grammatically follow the word which envisages the goal of the Cross, though logically they precede this, as the preparation for it.

[24] The only other reference to the humiliation of the Incarnation is the quite general thought of 2 Cor. viii. 9.

[25] The influence of Isa. liii. upon the Apostle's thought is also to be seen in such a phrase as 'delivered up for our trespasses' (Rom. iv. 25) and similar sayings (viii. 32; Eph. v. 2, 25; Gal. i. 4, ii. 20). In Rom. xv. 21, x. 16, he quotes Isa. lii. 15 and liii. 1 (cf. John xii. 38). His footnote to 1 Cor. xv. 3, 'Christ died for our sins according to the Scriptures,' would certainly have been Isa. liii. 4, 11, 12. Probably he and other Christians also found a prophecy of the Resurrection in the same context (cf. Weiss, *op. cit.*, p. 78). As examples of other New Testament references to Isa. liii., it is sufficient to mention Heb. ix. 28 ('having been once offered to bear the sins of many') and the prophecy of Caiaphas (John xi. 50). The reference to 'the lamb of God' (John i. 29, 36) is of doubtful bearing on our subject.

to be prepared for some recognition of the older meaning of the Songs, in substance, if not in form. This, in fact, is what we find in the New Testament idea of the Church as the new Israel, which is so closely linked to its Founder and Head, Jesus Christ. If we are to think of the ancient idea of the Servant as being capable of contraction and expansion (which was the point of the emphasis laid on corporate personality), then we may say that though the collective idea contracted into a primary reference to Jesus, yet its virtual presence is seen in the readiness with which it expanded into the doctrine of the Church. The very name 'Ecclesia', as Sohm has said,[26] implies a dogmatic judgment of value, for it denotes the new community of the covenant with God through or in Christ. It is not primarily a local community, though such a gathering of two or three in the name of Christ *is* the Ecclesia, nor is it numerically constructed from any union of such communities. The name carries on (through the usage of the Septuagint) the sense of corporate personality that had belonged to the 'congregation' of Israel (*Kahal*). Thus the Church is, as Lindsay says, 'a sacerdotal society':[27] 'the special function of the Church of Christ is to do in a better manner what the ancient Israel did imperfectly,' i.e. 'to approach God'.

'The main function of the New Testament Church is also to approach God. Just as in the Old Testament economy the priests when approaching God presented sacrifices to Him, so in the New Testament Church gifts are to be presented to God, and these gifts or offerings bear the Old Testament name of sacrifices. We are enjoined to present our *bodies*; our *praise*, "that is the fruit of our lips which make confession to His name"; our *faith*, our *almsgiving*;

[26] *Kirchenrecht*, Vol. I., pp. 10, 20.
[27] *The Church and the Ministry in the Early Centuries*, p. 34. Professor Box comments on the above: 'Was the conflict between the idea of nationality (Israel as a nation), and that of a religious community of a world mission ever harmonized, except, perhaps, in a sense in the N.T. idea of the new Israel, "the Israel of God"? Klausner (*Jesus of Nazareth*) is very illuminating on this point.' The reference is to the criticism which Klausner makes of the universalism of the teaching of Jesus as annulling Judaism as a life-force (e.g., p. 390).

our "doing good and communicating". These are all called "sacrifices" or "sacrifices well-pleasing to God," and to distinguish them from the offerings of the Old Testament economy, "spiritual or living sacrifices". The exertions made by St. Paul to bring the heathen to a knowledge of the Saviour are also called a sacrifice or offering. The New Testament Church is the ideal Israel, and does the work which the ancient Israel was appointed to do.'

As Canon A. J. Mason has said: 'The audacity of faith implied in the selection of the word [*ecclesia*] escapes us. . . . The fact . . . is a proof of their absolute confidence in the Lord Jesus and His Messiahship. The Israel according to the flesh, which rejected Him, and fulfilled the prophecies by rejecting Him, had forfeited all right to be considered the Israel of God. The right had passed to those who acknowledged Him.'[28] The creation of this new Israel, according to the Apostle who most fully elaborated the idea of the Church, is by the mystical faith-union with Him who first realized Israel's ideal. In Hort's words, ' Ideally the Ecclesia was co-extensive with humanity: all who shared the manhood which Christ had taken were potentially members of the Ecclesia: its ideals were identical with the ideals of a cleansed and perfected humanity.'[29]

It is neither necessary nor possible to examine here the familiar figures under which Paul has worked out this conception of the true Israel—the building of God, in which man's only claim is to be a humble fellow-worker with Him;[30] the family or household of God, having access through Christ in one Spirit unto the Father;[31] and especially the Body of Christ,[32] of which He is the Head, and all who are His are limbs or organs, sharing in His life. Such figures bring out the corporate personality of the Church, which is the key-thought to the Songs of the Servant of Yahweh. It is significant that the companion portrait to that of the Songs, the

[28] In *The Early History of the Church and the Ministry*, edited by H. B. Swete, p. 7.
[29] *The Christian Ecclesia*, p. 142.
[30] I Cor. iii. 9; cf. Eph. ii. 18 f.
[31] Eph. ii. 18, 19.
[32] Eph. iv. 4, etc.

portrait of Zion as the Wife of Yahweh, also figures in the Apostle's imagery of the Church: 'Husbands, love your wives, even as Christ also loved the Church and gave Himself up for it.'[33] The same dominating thought underlies the idea of the Church in the Fourth Gospel—both in the figure of the Vine and its branches, where the national emblem of Israel receives a new application to the new Israel, and in the idea of the Spirit continuing the work of Christ after His Ascension through the community He has created. Through all these conceptions there runs, either explicitly or implicitly, the fundamental experience of a *koinonia*, or fellowship of the Spirit, which is the life-breath of the new Israel. We recognize it in the brotherly intercourse of the primitive community of Jerusalem,[34] or in the contribution made by the Gentile Christians to the needs of their fellow-members at Jerusalem;[35] in the welcoming grasp of the hand or the practical sympathies of helpfulness and ministry.[36] Its secret is that it is created by the Holy Spirit;[37] it is a fellowship with Christ, and therefore with the Father.[38] To know the meaning of this most characteristic word *koinonia* is to enter into the rarer secrets as well as into the common life of the New Testament Christian; it is to breathe that purer air in which all things are possible, and a new vitality gives a new vigour to the limbs —for they are the limbs of Christ. But the pathway into that understanding is by the very conception that underlies the Songs of the Servant—the corporate personality in which the individual loses himself in some larger entity, to discover himself again on a higher level. That loss and that discovery are both expressed in the striking phrase used by the Apostle, 'the fellowship of His sufferings,' and by other words which amplify the same thought and experience: 'Now I rejoice in my sufferings for your sake, and fill up on my part that which is lacking of the afflictions of Christ in my flesh for his body's sake, which is the church.'[39] Perhaps no New Testament words serve to bring us more intimately into the historical

[33] Eph. v. 25.   [34] Acts ii. 42.
[35] Rom. xv. 26; cf. 2 Cor. viii. 4, ix. 13.
[36] Gal. ii. 9; Philem. 6; Heb. xiii. 16; Phil. i. 5.
[37] 2 Cor. xiii. 14; Phil. ii. 1.
[38] 1 Cor. i. 9, x. 16; 1 John i. 3, 6, 7.   [39] Phil. iii. 10; Col. i. 24.

meaning of the Songs of the Servant than do these. They have caught the iridescence of the blended personality, in which the distinction of 'mine' and 'thine' is not lost, but transcended to the enrichment of both. We catch this play of double colouring again in such words as 'always bearing about in the body the dying of Jesus, that the life also of Jesus may be manifested in our body.'[40]

4. Our study of the Servant of Yahweh in the Old and New Testaments has been exegetical, but Christian exegesis naturally leads on to Christian theology, and it is fitting to ask, in conclusion, what value these exegetical studies may have for a constructive statement of the work of Christ, and what light they throw on the nature of His Atonement. At least three important truths are emphasized when we approach the Atonement by this path, through its recognition of (1) the reality of history, (2) the corporate unity of the Church and its Head, and (3) the permanent place and value of sacrifice for sin.

(1) It has been one aim of the argument to bring out the natural continuity of the New Testament with the Old, and in particular the historical succession in which the devout and loyal members of Israel, old or new, stand to one another. This is most impressive in regard to the continuity of suffering which the service of God brings, as the price of spiritual loyalty. One great difficulty many have felt in regard to the Atonement is its apparent artificiality. God is conceived as allotting so much suffering for so much sin by a more or less arbitrary act. It is almost suggested that the allotment might have been other than it was, and some forms of the doctrine of Atonement have frankly made it turn on an acceptance of the offering at something beyond its intrinsic value.[41] Such artificialities are like those of a doctrine of 'miracle', which loses sight of second causes; unreality haunts every attempt of teleology to explain life too easily. If we want reality, we must pay its price in facing complexity and difficulty and, it

---

[40] 2 Cor. iv. 10. Note the use of 'delivered unto death' of the Apostle, in the following verse. Does this imply a reference to Christ's deliverance unto death? Cf. Rom. iv. 25, etc.

[41] E.g. Duns Scotus; cf. the article 'Acceptilation' in the *Encyclopædia of Religion and Ethics*, by R. S. Franks.

may be, unanswered questions. Emphasis has here been laid on the fact that the doctrine of the suffering of the Servant of Yahweh, both in the Old Testament and in the New, is an explanation of the fact of actual suffering, corporate or individual—suffering that is already there, and waiting explanation. Further, when we see that the suffering is actually incurred in the pursuit of a definite mission—as is the suffering of devout Israel, or of the Messiah-Servant in the New Testament —the suffering is partly explained by the intrinsic nature of things, that is of the world as we know it. Doubtless, this still leaves us with further philosophical and theological questions; but it is no small gain to approach these through the realities of history, and not through the speculations of a theory.

But when we use such a phrase as 'the realities of history', we already raise one of the most important and central of those questions. In what sense, from the standpoint of eternity, is history 'real'? Does all this intense consciousness of joy and sorrow, this passionate drama of interwoven lives, amount to no more than a foregone conclusion, the baseless fabric of a vision wrought before the eyes of some superhuman Prospero?[42] If we are not clear upon this issue, it is useless to discuss a particular example of the passion and pathos of life, called the Crucifixion, in its eternal meaning. But the insistent emphasis of both the Old Testament and of the New is upon the reality of human life, its cosmic significance. If Docetism is the first of Christian heresies, it is also the most promptly repudiated.[43] The reality of the atoning work of

---

[42] See Shakespeare's *Tempest*, Act IV., Scene i.
'These our actors,
As I foretold you, were all spirits, and
Are melted into air, into thin air;
And, like the baseless fabric of this vision,
The cloud-capp'd towers, the gorgeous palaces,
The solemn temples, the great globe itself,
Yea, all which it inherit, shall dissolve,
And, like this unsubstantial pageant faded,
Leave not a rack behind.'

[43] 1 John iv. 2. Docetism seems to have sprung from Gnostic dualism, not from issues proper to Christian thought (cf. Fortescue, in the *Encyclopædia of Religion and Ethics*, Vol. IV., p. 832).

Christ depends on the reality of His humanity. We are certainly aided in maintaining and understanding this when we approach Him as the greatest in the succession of those who actually realized the ideal of the Servant of Yahweh. Of course, this means the assertion of the reality of values as well as of events. It is in the spiritual meanings with which the 'events' of time are charged that their worth must lie for spiritual beings and for God Himself. The historic 'reality' of the Cross consists partly in the value which Christ and His disciples gave it.

(2) In the second place, the conception of the Servant of Yahweh prepares us for the corporate unity of the Church and its Head, a doctrine which is fundamental to any theory of the Atonement true to its New Testament data. In the Songs of the Servant, we have been led to recognize not an individual person, but a group, the corporate personality of Israel, now seen in its whole mixed mass, now contracting to the minority in whom its mission is actually being realized, or it may be to the one representative in whose consciousness alone it actually exists at any given moment of history. We have seen that such a group may be traced in the history of Judaism, before and after Jesus of Nazareth, but that in Him and in the new group which forms around Him there is a new and rich appropriation of the Servant's mission. It is the relation of the members of this group to Him which becomes so important, if the doctrine of the Atonement is to escape externality and mere transactionalism. It is quite true that a literal and prosaic interpretation of the fifty-third of Isaiah might insist—indeed, has often insisted—on penal substitution in its crudest form. But the point is that those who say, 'By His stripes we are healed' have already transcended any such external relation, and have been (spiritually) brought into the commonwealth of Israel, to be part of the spoil and inheritance of the Servant. They have entered into the corporate personality of Israel, and henceforth share its aims and destinies. We may say the same thing of the atoning work of Christ. We cannot with any hope of success stand outside the sphere of its influence, and discuss in cold blood the value of the stripes for anybody or anything. The very point is that those to whom

the value is real are those who have been brought within the sphere of spiritual influence, those who have been prostrated with wonder and adoration, like the kings of the nations in the Old Testament prophecy—those who say with the Apostle not only 'Christ is crucified for me,' but 'I am crucified with Christ.' For Paul, this mystical relation of faith is the setting in which all his doctrines of justification and sanctification and redemption must be seen—or rather, we should say, the atmosphere in which these doctrines alone can live. Now, faith-mysticism of this kind is the New Testament equivalent, on a higher spiritual level, of the ancient doctrine of corporate personality. It takes the emphasis off the individual life, and sees Christ as the centre of a new or rather renewed mankind, to which the believer belongs—yet it recognizes that the right to claim relation with the centre belongs only to those who actually stand within the circumference, those who can say, 'I live, and yet no longer I, but Christ liveth in me.' In other words, there is the actuality of the Servant's life in every member of the group. To Jesus Christ belongs a unique Saviourhood—yet to be saved by Him means to be made saviours of men. If all men, including Him who shared our humanity, are in some sense bound together in the solidarity of the race, then there is community in the responsibility for moral evil, as there is community in the benefit and enrichment of the race through moral good. The difference is that what we share racially, God in Christ shared voluntarily and vicariously. If what is wrong with our social conditions to-day is due to our excessive individualism and the consequent selfishness of much of our attitude and conduct towards others, it may be equally true that the inadequacy of our doctrines of Atonement is due to the same fault. Neither sin nor salvation can be defined in individualistic terms, though both of them involve an individual relation to God.

(3) Finally, and most important of all, there remains the question of the suffering of the Servant and its precise place and value in the ultimate scheme of things. This means something more than the efficacy of His mission, and the appeal of His suffering. The nations are moved to penitence by the spectacle of that suffering together with the vindication of

the sufferer, and that moral effect is part of the fulfilment of the mission. But it is not the whole of that mission. The suffering of the Servant is sacrificial and vicarious, so that through it these others can approach God, and are themselves accepted. So with the Cross of Christ, there is an effect wrought on men by seeing the Cross and seeing it in the light of its history, which is largely independent of the precise theory of the value of the sufferings. Men are, as a matter of fact, brought to God through Christ along most diverse lines of interpretation of the Cross, and often without any articulate theory at all. But it remains true that we cannot help asking the further question why the suffering of the good should be necessary thus to save the evil. It is the law of life as we know it, and it links us together in a social solidarity which for good or evil we cannot evade. The Cross of Christ is a central example of such suffering, historically unique in operation. How does it give us the peace with God, the confidence of approach to Him, the subtle blending of a deeper consciousness of sin with a higher vision of God's grace? If we try to state the ground of our confidence in positive terms, and in modern terms, we shall speak of the values of personality with which the world is enriched. *That which sin takes away from the world's worth, the Cross brings back, not in a fiction, but actually and really*, in the Servant perfect and individual, in the Servant-Church, imperfect and collective. Yet when we ask how one life, however heroic and sacrificial, can have such unique value, we seem to be driven further back still to a conception of that life which shall see it as unique in source, the conception of Jesus Christ as God manifest in the flesh, manifest as in no other life of man. But what is this, but to assert the kinship of God and man, and to reassert the covenant between Yahweh and Israel, which lies behind the fifty-third of Isaiah? That covenant was sacrificial, for the loyalty of love that bound Yahweh to Israel meant suffering for God from which He did not shrink. It is not said, yet it must be implied, that Yahweh suffers in the suffering of His Servant, as Yahweh triumphs in His Servant's vindication. In a sense, of course, both are human metaphors—yet they stand for a vital truth. In spite of much Church doctrine, an

H

impassible God is as impossible as a docetic Christ. In the last resort, the sacrifice is God's, and corporate personality attains its supreme achievement in the sacrificial realization of the kinship of man and God. The final appeal of grace is in the suffering *God*, as the final depth of sin is the churlishness that scorns such grace. We may see in the Servant of Yahweh the portrait not only of Jesus of Nazareth, but of the Eternal God in His most salient attribute of covenantal and sacrificial suffering.

> ' I think this is the authentic sign and seal
> Of Godship, that it ever waxes glad,
> And more glad, until gladness blossoms, bursts,
> Into a rage to suffer for mankind,
> And recommence at sorrow : drops like seed. . . .
> And thence rise, tree-like grow through pain to joy,
> More joy and most joy,—do man good again.'[44]

[44] R. Browning, *Balaustion's Adventure*, Vol. I., p. 654 (ed. 1896).

III

THE CROSS OF JEREMIAH

PREFACE

THIS study of personal religion contains four lectures delivered in Oxford, at the Vacation Term of Biblical Study (1924), and is of similar character to that on *The Cross of Job*, published in 1916. At some later date I hope to complete these elementary studies in the Old Testament religion by two others, on *The Cross of the Servant of Jehovah*, and *The Cross of the Psalmists*, in order to bring out the continuity of the New Testament with the Old Testament, and the cogency of the modern 'argument from prophecy', when based on undogmatic historical exegesis. The student of Jeremiah is fortunate in having so many helps to the understanding of the book, and in particular, Dr. Skinner's fine work on *Prophecy and Religion*. To this I am of course indebted, especially in making translations of the passages quoted. I have also to thank Professor A. J. D. Farrer, B.A., and the Rev. C. M. Hardy, B.A., for useful criticism of the typescript in general.

The study of Jeremiah is the best approach to the noblest conceptions of fellowship with God which the Old Testament contains, themselves the true preparation for the deeper understanding of the New Testament.

H. WHEELER ROBINSON

Regent's Park College
N.W.8
    September, 1925

'ONE day in the month of September I went down the *khud*, and standing on the bridge of a river, was filled with wonder to see the indomitable strength and playful whirls of its currents. Oh! how pure and white its waters! Why then does it dash downwards in order to deprive itself of this purity? The lower it goes, the more will it become defiled and tainted by the dirt and refuse of this earth. Why, then, does it rush headlong in that very direction? But what power has it to keep still for its own sake? By command of that All-ruling One, though it be stained with the dirt of the earth, still it has to humble its pride and take a downward course, in order to fertilize the land, make it yield grain.

'I was musing thus, when suddenly I heard the solemn commandment of the Guide within me: "Give up thy pride, and be lowly like this river. The truth thou hast gained, the devotion and trustfulness that thou hast learnt here, go, make them known to the world." I was startled! Must I then turn back from this holy land of the Himalayas? . . . It was God's command that I should go back home; could man's will hold out against that? . . . His will was my law. Harmonizing my will with His, I made ready to go home.' Devendranath Tagore, *Autobiography*, pp. 261-263.

'Dispone et ordina omnia secundum tuum velle et videre, et non invenies, nisi semper aliquid pati debere, aut sponte aut invite et ita crucem semper invenies.' A Kempis, *De Imitatione Christi*, II. 12, 3.

'Rien n'est perdu quand on l'offre.' Bourget, *Le Sens de la Mort*, p. 310.

'It is as if there were a cross unseen, standing on its undiscovered hill, far back in the ages, out of which were sounding always, just the same deep voice of suffering love and patience, that was heard by mortal ears from the sacred hill of Calvary.' Horace Bushnell, *The Vicarious Sacrifice*, p. 31.

CONTENTS

IV. THE CROSS ABOVE—*the man's God*   174

(a) Theology on a historical basis; the Bible a source-book, not a text-book. The originality of Jeremiah not in formal doctrine but in religious experience.

(b) Sin a wrong to man's true nature, the act of the individual *will*; hence the futility of external worship and the need for an inner consecration. The hardening of habit as one penalty of sin. The heart known to God.

(c) The life of trust, and the 'natural' working of God's wrath against sin. Sin is against grace (ingratitude). God's patient love, and sorrow through man's sin—the cross God carries. His New Covenant. The future lay with the exiles in Babylon. The happy return to God.

(d) The influence of Jeremiah in (1) the personal religion of the Psalms, (2) the sacrificial suffering of the Servant, (3) the 'Job' problem of the suffering of the innocent. Their synthesis as an approach to the Cross of Christ.

I

THE RECORD OF THE CROSS

'SOME men's failures,' as George Macdonald has said, 'are eternities beyond other men's successes.' It was so with Amiel. As he wrote down his sombre story of a spirit conscious of its failure to achieve anything worthy of its gifts, as he wrote his epitaph in the words, ' All that can be, must come to be, and what does not come to be was nothing,' he did not know that his success was to be the record of his failure and that his *Journal Intime* was to become a classic of autobiography. It was so with Jeremiah. When he tried to arrest the course of a nation, only to be thrown down and trampled underfoot, when he cried out in bitterness of heart against the inexorable Will that compelled a poet to become a prophet, and a lover of men to be counted their enemy, he little knew that the development and record of his own lonely experience of failure was to be a success of the highest rank and influence. For if we want to know the meaning of personal religion at its finest and highest in the Old Testament, we must become, like Baruch, disciples of Jeremiah. In this respect there is no figure comparable with his, nor any of whom the revelation is so intimate and full. The only parallel within the Bible is the Apostle Paul. If religion means at last fellowship with God—and what else can it mean?—then Jeremiah can both show and tell more of it than any other under the Old Covenant—and did he not see from afar the New? Other prophets had their place and portion, and their measure of success; it was with him as with the poet in Schiller's poem, who thought of God whilst others secured His gifts, and so had nothing left but—God Himself.

' I sat alone because of Thy hand.' The penalty of leadership is loneliness. The tourist may travel in a well-marked track, for he goes where others have been before him; the explorer opens the way to some distant goal, which he alone can see. The life of Jeremiah would have been a lonely one simply as the pioneer of religious truth and its moral application, but, as the prophet of personal religion, the very essence and nature of his contribution was to consist in its loneliness, so far as fellowship with men was concerned. He was to show that religion did not in the last resort mean the sacrifices of the altar, the worship of the temple, the covenant of a written law, but that it was a personal fellowship with God, to which all these were at the best mere accessories, and at the worst, delusive distractions. He was to be driven back on God, because men failed him, and by that very experience to discover and to reveal what it meant to have God. He was to illustrate the famous works of Augustine, which have rightly won a Scriptural dignity—his was to be the unquiet heart, which knew no rest until it found rest in God.

Human personality is a most subtle blending of individual and social factors. One of the most obvious lessons of history is the alternation of these factors, according as one or other of them has received predominant emphasis. It is so to-day when we have passed from satisfaction with industrial individualism to some sense of social responsibility and corporate life. It was so, but in the reverse direction, in the times of Jeremiah. In him we see the beginnings of the reaction from the thought of the nation or the family as the unit in religion to that of the individual life, which the later prophet Ezekiel was to elaborate; it is through Jeremiah that we first hear that proverbial complaint of the people, 'The fathers have eaten sour grapes and the children's teeth are set on edge' (xxxi. 29). This relative individualism of Jeremiah does not, of course, mean a complete detachment. If we compare his attitude with ours, still largely individualistic, Jeremiah was far more conscious than we are of the corporate or social solidarity of life. But the new thing he had to bring men was the discovery of an individual relation to God within that common social relationship, the discovery of something previously unrealized. It is the tension created by the new claim in conflict with the old that leads to the sufferings, moral and physical, of the prophet Jeremiah. His cross was borne for others, as every cross, in

the Christian sense, must be borne. Men owe what they are
to the society into which they were born; if they rise to the
fulness of their manhood, they will pay that debt. The
millionaire's gift of a public park is one way, and a good way,
of paying it; the quality of a good day's work by artist or
artisan is another. But the finest repayment of all is that of
one who lifts his fellows nearer to the source of all good,
by being lifted up upon a cross. That was the way of Jesus
Christ, and, in his own degree, that was the way of his forerunner and prototype, Jeremiah.

There are four principal ways of studying our subject, and
they are like concentric circles. We begin with the outermost
of all, the literary record. We pass to the historical conditions
and external events of the prophet's life, which we learn from
this record. We penetrate still further, as this prophet beyond
any other enables us to do, into the psychological and ethical
and religious experience of his inner life. Finally, we stand
at the centre, or rather look up from it to a higher centre,
in asking what the whole experience tells us about God. First
the Book, second the History, third the Man, and fourth the
Man's God.

What impression would be made by the present Book of
Jeremiah on a reader who came to it for the first time, eager
to test the truth of these great claims for the prophet? Let
us imagine him trying to read it through, as he would any
other English book of to-day. The first chapter would be intelligible and interesting, telling as it does of God's call to the
prophet in his youth, and the young man's shrinking from so
great a task, and describing the vision of the early blossoming
tree, which became a symbol to him of God's activity; just as
Brother Lawrence tells us in his *Practice of the Presence of
God* that 'seeing a tree stripped of its leaves, and considering
that within a little time the leaves would be renewed, and
after that the flowers and fruit appear, he received a high view
of the providence and power of God, which has never since
been effaced from his soul'. The second vision in the same
chapter, of the pot boiling over, would also be intelligible; it
represents the overflow of some unnamed people from the
north who shall invade the prophet's land, or else the kindling

of a fire from the north beneath Judah itself. The main theme of the second following chapters would also be apparent, for the prophet is telling his people why this judgment is about to come upon them. But this reproach of the people for disloyalty to God would soon become monotonous to the ordinary reader, for there is no obvious development of the thought, as we usually expect in a book, and the connection of one passage with another is not at all obvious. The prophet seems to be saying the same thing over and over again; in fact we are reading extracts from a number of sermons and addresses (without any definite clue to their order or topic), interspersed with highly emotional outcries on the part of the prophet himself. If our reader were of the steadfast sort, not lightly abandoning a task once undertaken, he might get as far as the thirteenth chapter, and find the prophet engaging in some strange symbolism with a girdle, or even as far as the eighteenth, where there is a visit to the potter, working a lower wheel with his feet, whilst his hands swiftly mould the clay on the upper revolving wheel, and the nineteenth, where again there is an act of prophetic symbolism, the breaking of an earthenware pot. But nothing has happened, so far, of any account, and the reader might be pardoned for an instinctive gratitude, in reading the twentieth chapter, that something should happen at long last, even though it is that Jeremiah is beaten and put into the stocks. This is all that has been told of his life since his call under Josiah; yet, in the twenty-first chapter, we find ourselves in the reign of Zedekiah, and the prophet is an old man, with the siege and destruction of Jerusalem close at hand. But, in the twenty-fifth chapter, we are carried back some sixteen years into the reign of Jehoiakim. I think our puzzled reader would before this have stolen a glance at the end to see how many more chapters there were, and to learn, perhaps with dismay, that there were as many as there are weeks in the year. But now that we have got to the crest of the hill, the path downwards would be much easier. From the twenty-sixth chapter onwards to the forty-fifth, there are narratives with a few sermons, instead of sermons with very little narrative. The story of the prophet becomes that of a Passion, interwoven with the fortunes of

Jerusalem itself, until he is taken to Egypt by some of his countrymen, and all sight of him is lost. The character of the book again changes at the forty-sixth chapter, where begin a number of detached prophecies about foreign nations. If our student had been reading the Greek version of the Septuagint, instead of the English which follows the Hebrew order, this bundle of prophecies would have been found at the middle of the book (between xxv. 13 and 15), and not at the end. The last chapter of all is an extract from the Book of Kings, describing the fall of Jerusalem.

It is worth while to take such a preliminary glance at the book, however familiar it may be to us, if only to remind us of the difficulties in the way of a real appreciation of the prophet's work. Fortunately, a great deal can be done to remove those difficulties; indeed, we know more about the composition of this book than of any other of the 'Prophets'. We can see how Jeremiah's spoken words first came to be written down by the prophet's secretary, Baruch, so as to become the nucleus of the present work; how additions were made to it, including eventually those narratives about the prophet, which may reasonably be assigned to Baruch; how to these were added the 'foreign' prophecies (few, if any, of which are by Jeremiah), which now stand at different places in the two versions, Hebrew and Greek; how, finally, the closing chapter was borrowed from another book, because it seemed fitting that the story of a prophet so intimately linked with the fall of Jerusalem should contain an account of that event.

The starting-point for this literary analysis is given us by the graphic account in the thirty-sixth chapter. The defeat of the Egyptians by the Babylonians at Carchemish in 605 no doubt influenced Jeremiah in his conviction that the time was ripe for a prophet's testimony (cf. xlvi. 2-12). But this testimony was to take a new form. Hitherto it has been oral, now it is to be written and read out to the people by Baruch, his companion and scribe. Except in manner of delivery and particular application, it is no new message, but the gathering up of what Jeremiah has been saying for the last twenty-two years. He dictates these old prophecies to Baruch, leading up to the logical climax that the new power from the north, the Babylonians, would surely accomplish that vengeance of Yahweh on the sins of the people which the prophet had once expected at the hands of the Scythians, or some other northern hordes. The roll was read on a fast day, when there were many to hear. News of it was brought from the temple above to a room of the royal palace below, where a number of state officials were gathered. The serious way in which they received it shows how great was the place a prophet's word could take in the national life. They feel bound to tell the king, Jehoiakim, but the precaution they take shows that they have rightly measured his attitude, for they bid Baruch and his master go into hiding. Then the roll of papyrus is read to the king, as he sits on that winter's day by the brazier. His anger compromises with his curiosity, for again and again, as the reader completes three or four columns of the roll, the king snatches it from him and slashes off the unrolled and read portion with the scribe's penknife, and flings it into the burning brazier, till all is read and all has been destroyed. The timely precaution of the officials prevents the ordered arrest of Baruch and Jeremiah, who, nothing daunted, proceed to the dictation and writing of another roll like the first. But it is significant that we read of an expansion of the earlier words: 'there were added besides unto them many like words'. It is evident that Baruch's roll became the nucleus of the present Book of Jeremiah, and it is of interest to ask what it contained.

The roll contained *prophecies*, not narratives such as are found in the present book of Jeremiah. This is clear from the practical use to be made of it, which is to bring the people to repentance when they hear of the evil that Yahweh is about to bring upon them; it is also clear from the explicit statement that the roll is to contain all the words which He has spoken to Jeremiah. It would naturally be written in the first person, since the original speaker is dictating. It would include only those prophecies which Jeremiah remembered, out of his activity for the previous twenty-two years, i.e. from 626, when he was called to prophesy, until 604, when the roll was written. It would be short enough to be read through without break, and we know that it was so read three times within a few hours. These are sufficient tests to ascertain substantially what the first Book of Jeremiah contained. We shall look for it chiefly within the first twenty-five chapters, for these are prophecies, and there is little narrative. These prophecies are also reported in the first person. They are concerned largely with the irreligious state of the nation, and the coming judgment through invaders. This ' foe from the north ' expected by the prophet according to his earliest utterances could not then have been the Babylonians, but was probably the Scythians; but it was natural that in 604, when the Babylonians, after their victory over the Egyptians at Carchemish, were first coming into the arena of Palestine, Jeremiah should make a new identification. The prophets stood for principles, not for the details of their application, and the principles of 626 received a new application in 604.

But it is also clear, from what has been said, that the roll of Baruch could not have contained all that now stands in the first half of the Book of Jeremiah. For example, there is a lament over Jehoahaz (Shallum), the successor of Jehoiakim, who was exiled to Egypt (xxii. 10-12), and another over the fate of Jehoiachin and his mother, who were involved in the capture of Jerusalem in 597—that is seven years after the roll was written (xii. 18, 19; cf. 2 Kings xxiv. 8, 15). There is an answer given by the prophet to Zedekiah, the last king of Jerusalem, in 588 (xxi. 1-10), and a prophecy relating to him and to the Jews deported in the first exile, in 597 (xxiv.). Then there are undated prophecies, which reveal by their style and contents that they belong to a period later than that of the roll. In the tenth chapter (1-16), there is an attack on idols, suggesting the times and perhaps the influence of Deutero-Isaiah, the prophet of the exile. In the seventeenth chapter (19-27) there is an exhortation to honour the Sabbath, which seems to belong to the age of Nehemiah. As to the autobiographical pieces, which throw such a wonderful light on the prophetic consciousness of Jeremiah, it is difficult to say whether they would stand in this first roll, but the probabilities seem strongly against it. It was no concern of anybody then to know how much it had cost the prophet to prophesy, when his one mission was to proclaim judgment in the name of Yahweh.

It is, however, probable that the roll contained the first part of the twenty-fifth chapter, perhaps as its pungent conclusion : [1]

'Since the thirteenth year of Josiah, son of Amon, king of Judah, to this day, for three and twenty years, I have spoken to you early and often, saying, "Turn you every one from his evil way and from the wickedness of your actions: thus shall ye dwell in the land which Yahweh has given to you and your fathers for ever and ever." But you have not listened to me. Therefore Yahweh has spoken thus: "Forasmuch as 'you have not listened to My words, I send and take a people from the North, and bring it against this land and its inhabitants, and all the peoples round about it. I will lay them waste, and make them a perpetual desolation and hissing and reproach; I will banish from them the sound of joy and the sound of mirth, the voice of the bridegroom and the voice of the bride, the sound of the mill stones and the light of the lamp. And they shall serve among the nations seventy years. Thus will I bring upon this land all My words which I have spoken against it, even all that is written in this book."'

This was undoubtedly the central theme of the roll, for it is summarized in the words of the King Jehoiakim, when he had heard it, 'Why hast thou written, saying, The king of Babylon shall certainly come and destroy this land, and shall cause to cease from thence man and beast?' (xxxvi. 29).

It is worth while to dwell on such details or literary criticism, not because the roll of Baruch can ever be any more than a piece of theoretical reconstruction, but because the effort to work it out shows us so much of the way in which Scripture came into being. Because the oral message has failed, the written record of it is made, and this becomes the nucleus of other records. Already we have seen that the second edition of the roll was longer than the first, and that many new words

[1] Here given largely as restored by Skinner and others, on the basis of the LXX (pp. 240, 241).

(perhaps remembered for the first time by the prophet) were now recorded. The very fact that we are thrown back on a prophet's memory of twenty-two years' work shows us that verbal accuracy is not the chief thing in Scripture.

Even without the statement that 'many like words' were added to those of the first roll, the present book would have shown us with sufficient clearness how the roll was expanded. Our preliminary glance at the contents of the book has shown us that its character changes from the twenty-sixth chapter onwards, and that we have now narratives with some prophecies, instead of prophecies with little narrative. Indeed, from the thirty-seventh to the forty-fourth chapters, we have what might be called a biography of the prophet, which it is natural to ascribe to his secretary, Baruch, as the only man with both the skill and the opportunity to give us such an account. It is significant that this section of the book closes with the short forty-fifth chapter, which is a personal prophecy given for the comfort of Baruch himself, a natural close for an account of the prophet from Baruch's pen. This biography, which may have been originally more extensive (portions of it apparently stand in earlier parts of the book) is our second main source, side by side with the original roll of dictated prophecies. We have an interesting opportunity of comparing the two sources in the fact that a particular event is described in both of them. In the roll of prophecies, Jeremiah recorded a message given him to deliver at the gate of the temple, a rebuke of the false confidence of Yahweh's worshippers in the mere possession of this block of buildings belonging to Yahweh, and therefore immune from peril. Yahweh, says the prophet, desires social justice, moral conduct, and whole-hearted worship. He will not allow His temple to become like some cave that shelters robbers; He will destroy it, as He formerly destroyed the temple of Shiloh (vii. 1-15). This is the substance of the famous temple-sermon, which is so characteristic of the new emphasis of the prophet on personal religion. But we are told nothing of its date or setting or of the effect produced by it. The prophet is content simply to recall what he said. His biographer, however, has given us in a much later chapter (xxvi.) the story of that sermon from a spectator's standpoint, and has made us realize how much we lose in being ignorant of the exact historical background of so many prophetic messages. Baruch tells us that the message was given at the beginning of Jehoiakim's reign, i.e. in 608, or four years before the incident of the roll itself. The message is given much more briefly than in chapter vii.: unless the people obey Yahweh, He will destroy the temple, as He did that of Shiloh, and make the city an example of a curse. But the sequel of the prophet's words is given at full length. Such a declaration against the proud inviolability of the temple is nothing less than a blasphemy against Yahweh; it is incredible that Yahweh can ever have given such a word as this. Jeremiah is accordingly brought by the priests and other prophets before the secular authorities, ' the princes of Judah,' and his death demanded. Jeremiah's defence is that he has simply spoken that which he has been told to speak, and his plea is accepted by the princes. Then certain elders rise in the assembly and recall the similar instance of Micah's prophesying against Jerusalem in the time of Hezekiah, without harm being done to him; indeed, those who then heard Micah were brought to repentance by his message. It is plain from the story that Jeremiah was not without friends in high places, as, indeed, we have seen from the desire of these secular authorities that he and Baruch should escape the king's wrath at the reading of the roll.

A modern editor, desiring to publish the Book of Jeremiah for the first time, would probably given us Baruch's biography of the prophet by way of introduction, followed by the prophecies either in their strictly chronological order, or arranged topically, with footnotes to indicate the dates at which they were delivered. But whatever hand or hands have shaped our present Book, the result is very different. The prophecies come first, and most of the biography second, and the order is far from being chronological, nor can any topical arrangement be detected, except here and there, as in the short collection of prophecies about successive kings (xxii. 1-xxiii. 8). We cannot suppose that Baruch himself would have written so shapeless a Book; moreover, there is clear proof that later hands than his have been at work upon it. For one thing, there is the appendix, taken verbatim from the second Book of Kings (lii.), which refers to the release of Jehoiachin in 561, and therefore brings down the date at which the chapter was added to this Book to a time when Baruch must have been dead. More important than this, we have the group of foreign prophecies, forming a third main source of the Book, at present to be read in the Hebrew version in chapters xlvi.-li., i.e. at the close of Baruch's biography. In the Greek version, however, which is considerably shorter than the Hebrew, these foreign prophecies are not only in a different order, but they are read in quite a different place. They follow xxv. 13, just where we have seen reason to believe that the roll of prophecies left off, so that they follow the words ' which Jeremiah hath prophesied against all the nations '. It is on the whole more likely that this was the original place of the addition, but that in the Hebrew version the whole section has at some period been transferred to the end of Baruch's biography, instead of standing as it does in the Greek, at the end of Baruch's roll of prophecies.

As to these foreign prophecies, it is quite clear that some of them cannot be by Jeremiah. The very long prophecy against Babylon (l.-li. 58) pre-supposes the destruction of Jerusalem as a relatively remote event (l. 28, li. 11, 51), the coming deliverance through Cyrus, and an attitude towards Babylon altogether different from that of Jeremiah. The prophecy against Moab (xlviii.) is almost certainly later than Jeremiah, and incorporates parts of Isaiah xv. f., an elegy of the fifth century. How much of the rest may be Jeremianic is a difficult question to decide. The prophecies against Egypt (xlvi., Carchemish), against Philistia (xlvii.) and against Edom (xlix. 7 f.) are defended by some modern scholars, whilst others reject all. But there is no good reason for doubting that Jeremiah did prophesy about the other nations surrounding Israel, and beneath some of these oracles may well lie original words of his, which have been subsequently expanded to meet the needs of new generations of readers.

The literary forms of the present Book of Jeremiah are both poetry and prose, and there is no reason to doubt that both go back to the prophet's utterances, independently of the prose narratives of Baruch. The alternation is aptly compared by George Adam Smith with ' canoe voyages in Canada, in which the canoe now glides down a stream and is again carried overland by what are called portages to other streams or other branches of the same stream' (*Jeremiah*, p. 37). It is worth while for us to consider the significance of the predominance of poetry in the Bible. It is to be found not only in such poetical books as the Psalms and Job, but in the prose-poems of the early chapters of Genesis, the parables of Jesus, the visions of apocalyptists, and supremely in the oracles of prophets. The poetic form of the Bible is essential to its truth, for religion itself is the poetry of life. As Everard Meynell says, in his *Life of Francis Thompson*, ' Song, like Prayer, is for ever re-stating and re-establishing the permanent values' (p. 288). Government Reports will tell us in prose the extent of the catch of herrings in a season, but we go to poetry, like ' Caller Herrin'' or 'Three Fishers went sailing', to give us the higher truth, the humanities of the fishing industry. Jeremiah was doubly a poet, first by nature and temperament, but then also by the religious conventions of his time, which made poetry or rhythmic prose the vehicle of divine revelation. It was not only that the poetic form made such utterances easier to be remembered by both prophet and people (a fact which makes Jeremiah's memory of the prophecies of twenty years more explicable). There was also the consciousness that the poetic form was more suited to the utterance of religious truth. There is a close parallel here with the procedure in regard to divine oracles amongst other peoples. Take the best known of all, the Delphic or Pythian oracle. The prophetess, after drinking water from the sacred spring, seated herself upon the tripod in the inner shrine over the cleft from which vapour arose. She spoke in ecstasy, under the influence, as was supposed, of Apollo, who knew the will of Zeus. Probably none but the professional interpreters understood her utterance— we may think of the similar ' gift of tongues' in the Corinthian Church, also needing interpretation. These interpreters translated the oracle given through the Pythia into verse, usually hexameters, and as such it was given out. Here we see the same conception of poetry as the proper vehicle for divine revelation. Was there a closer parallel? Was there anything in Hebrew prophecy corresponding to the ecstatic condition of the Pythia, in which the oracular message was first conceived? If we went back to the earliest forms of Hebrew 'prophecy' so-called, there certainly was. The band of prophets whom Saul met, by whose inspiration he was himself seized (1 Sam. x. 10-13), sufficiently shows this. But something of the same experience survived all through the history of Hebrew prophecy, though in the greater prophets it was driven from the centre to the circumference. The visions of an Amos, Isaiah's experience of the 'hand' of Yahweh (viii. 11), the trance states of Ezekiel (iii. 14, 15; iv. 4; viii.-xi.) are all part of this prophetic tradition, and without such an abnormal psychic experience, it seems probable that no man would have been recognized as a prophet. Jeremiah himself must have had such experiences, however true it is that in him more than in any other of the great prophets we see the advance from these cruder experiences towards spiritual communion with God in personal, ethical fellowship. The vision of the almond, or 'watcher' tree that told of Yahweh's watchfulness, or of the boiling pot that told of the northern peril, must have been objects conceived to exist actually before him by the act of the God who thus spoke to him. The inner compulsion that overpowered him, shrink as he might (xx. 9), was for him not simply a moral ideal, a sense of duty, but an intense psychic experience, in which the Spirit of Yahweh wrestled with his spirit—as an earlier age could conceive Yahweh in bodily form wrestling with Jacob. The message, for which he must sometimes wait a long time, however much he desired it (xlii. 7), was given or withheld in a way he could not consciously control. Perhaps the message when it did come was some brief sentence, or even a word, like the word 'Watcher', which sprang into his mind when he saw the almond tree. Perhaps it was a strong impulse inarticulate, like the impulse to go about with a yoke upon his neck (xxviii. 10), or to test the Rechabites by the offer of wine (xxxv. 2), or to hide amongst the rocks a waist-cloth he had worn (xiii. 1). In any case, the form in which his prophecies now chiefly exist must be conceived as a subsequent working up of the initial experience into articulate and explicit form. Whether in the more elaborate form of metre, or in the simpler form of more or less rhythmical prose, the prophet's interpretation of some experience of God essentially constitutes the message. Thus we may think of the prophet combining in himself the two parts of the Delphic procedure; he received the divine impulse, and he translated it into the conventional form of poetic expression. Or, if we like to take a characteristically modern illustration, we may think of the metal selenium, which, as the physicists tell us, shows variations of electrical conductivity according to the degree of light that falls upon it; thus it can translate a ray of light into audible sounds by means of an inserted telephone, and even a blind man, using this selenium optophone, can read an ordinary newspaper.[2] So to the prophetic consciousness there came some ray of light from the unseen, some ineffable, unanalysable contact with Him who is Spirit, some communication not in human speech or human thought at all. But, in the responsive human soul, it set up currents of new life, necessarily translated, if they were ever to be understood by the prophet or his fellows, into the poetry or prose now before us. It is not necessary, indeed it is most unlikely, that the prophet himself was able to analyse the elements of his experience; often enough, words would leap into consciousness simultaneously with the first experience, and be heard from the beginning as spoken by the very lips of God. But whatever the psychological process by which we explain the experience, the explanation does not in any way detract from the truth of the content, or the reality of the inspiration.

Hebrew poetry has two marked characteristics, the first and the most important its parallelism, the second, its use of rhythmical stresses or ' beats '. The parallelism which is found in Hebrew poetry (to a degree found nowhere else except in Babylonian) consists in linking the sense of two lines, so that the second continues the thought of the first, either by repetition, or by supplement, or by direct antithesis. An example of the simplest form of parallelism in Jeremiah would be x. 23:

[2] *The Moon Element*, by Fournier D'Albe, 1924.

'I knów, O Yahwéh, that not mán's is his róad,
Not mán's as he wálks and fixés his stép.'

Here the second line virtually repeats the first; in both, the underlying thought is that man proposes and God disposes. Each of these parallel lines, moreover, has four 'beats' or rhythmical stresses. The number of syllables does not matter (within reasonable limits); it is the number of stresses that gives the quality to the verse. But far and away the favourite metre of Jeremiah is that known as the *Kinah*, or 'dirge', because this was used in lamentations for the dead, though its actual use extends widely beyond this. It consists of five beats, divided into a three and a two:

'Forgéts a máiden her órnaments, a bríde her gírdle?'
                                                    (ii. 32).

The effect of this will be seen from one of Jeremiah's most impressive lyrics—the dirge on Death the Reaper, of which someone has truly remarked that more could not be said in eight short lines:

'For Death has come up at our windows,
    Entered our palaces,
To cut off the child from the street
    And young men from the squares;
And the corpses of men have fallen,
    Like dung on the field,
And like the sheaves that are left by the reaper,
    With none to gather' (ix. 21, 22).

In the account the prophet gives of his call, poetry mingles with prose:

'This word of Yahweh came to me:—
    Before I shaped thee unborn I knew thee,
    And before thou camest from the womb I consecrated
        thee;
    For a prophet to the nations have I given thee.

And I said:
  Ah, Lord Yahweh!
  Behold I know not how to speak;
    For I am (only) a youth.

But Yahweh said to me:
  Do not say " I am (only) a youth "
    For whithersoever I send thee thou shalt go,
    And whatsoever I command thee thou shalt speak.
  Do not fear before them, for I am with thee to rescue
      thee:
    —an oracle of Yahweh.

Then Yahweh put forth His hand and touched my mouth
    and
Yahweh said to me:—
  Lo, I put My words in thy mouth:
  See, I appoint thee this day
    Over the nations and over the kingdoms
    To uproot and to pull down, to build up and to plant.'

Or, again, an oracle may be recorded in prose, though of more
or less rhythmic character:

  'Then Yahweh said to me: " Do not pray on behalf of
  this people for good; when they fast, I am not listening to
  their crying, and when they offer burnt-offering and meal-
  offering, I am not accepting them, for with sword and
  famine and pestilence I consume them "' (xiv. 11, 12).

But it is in the poetry of the book that its chief treasures
lie, and that poetry takes the form of the religious lyric which
is Israel's great æsthetic achievement. As in Jeremiah the
stream of Israel's personal religion deepens that it may at last
broaden into the piety of the Psalter, to which he has contri-
buted so much, so we may recognize in him also one of Israel's
genuine artists in the one form of art which Israel's religion
permitted—the religious lyric.

II

THE CROSS WITHOUT

Do men make events, or events make men? It has been said that 'the pyschical events which take place in men form the real kernel of history'.[1] The personal life of Jeremiah will illustrate this truth, for the finest religious development of the future was already anticipated in his experience, and his personal influence ultimately became a principal factor in the guidance of this development. But the one truth must not blind us to the other which is its complement—that these psychical events are never divorced from the contemporary life of their times. If psychical events are the kernel, then external events are the shell, without which the kernel could not grow. In particular, the personal life and teaching of the prophets of Israel is most closely inter-related with the social and political environment of their work. A man cannot even exist in a vacuum, much less prophesy in it. The prophet, like the poet, must know the throb and thrill of a real experience before he has anything to interpret; his soul needs the stimulus of national and international life around him. Except for Homer, we should know little or nothing of the Homeric age; but then without the Homeric age or its equivalent, we should have had no Homer. Just as it is true that without the material and spiritual expansion of the Elizabethan age, Shakespeare would not be Shakespeare, so is it true that without the sorrows of Judah's closing generation religion would have been impoverished by the loss of the greatest of Hebrew prophets—Jeremiah.

It is, therefore, no accident that for three-quarters of a century after the last appearance of Isaiah no prophet's voice was heard upon the hills of Judah. Then, within the last

[1] Sigwart, *Logic*, ii. 441, quoted by Galloway, *The Principles of Religious Development*, p. 17.

quarter of the seventh century, the silence was broken by no less than four contemporary prophets, Zephaniah, Jeremiah, Nahum and Habakkuk, whilst that same generation saw the first serious attempt to realize earlier prophetic ideals of social morality and worship in the Deuteronomic Reformation. The flow of prophetic utterance which thus followed its ebb was like that of all artistic creation, which does not come to a man's mere wish, or even because of his earnest striving. For the first three-quarters of the century, the national life of Judah was lived in both political and religious bondage to Assyria. The term ' political ', in fact, usually meant ' religious ' for ancient life and thought. When Judah became Assyria's vassal, as it did in the seventh century, this meant that the Assyrian gods acquired a new meaning in the eyes of the ordinary Israelite; had they not given to the Assyrian his military supremacy? The Israelite of those days had not attained to the rigorous monotheism of the later Judaism; even the great prophets themselves had not explicitly formulated their virtual monotheism. The average man was still quite ready for such a compromise as that of the East Anglian king named by Bede, who naïvely erected a pagan and a Christian altar side by side in his royal temple (*Ecc. Hist.*, ii. 15). That was, in fact, the policy pursued by Manasseh, who was king of Judah during half of the seventh century. Doubtless, it was politically expedient to honour the religion of his Assyrian over-lord, but we need not disbelieve in his sincerity, because he thought the worship of Yahweh compatible with the worship of the Assyrian gods. We read that ' he built altars for all the host of heaven in the two courts of the house of Yahweh ' (2 Kings xxi. 5, cf. xxiii. 12). This is a reference to the astrological religion for which Babylon and (through Babylon) Assyria are famous. In the Assyrio-Babylonian pantheon, the sun, moon and planets were identified with leading gods. Manasseh also revived or continued the cult of the ' high places ' which had been attacked by the eighth-century prophets, and had suffered some discouragement under Manasseh's father, Hezekiah. The fanaticism of Manasseh even went to the length of sacrificing his own child by fire. The general result of Manasseh's policy was, therefore, much the same as that of Ahab and Jezebel,

when they introduced the Phœnician Baal—to reduce Yahweh
to one member of a pantheon, even though the chief one, to
treat Him no longer as a jealous God, and ultimately to degrade
His worship to the level of the nature-cults of Canaan.

That this was the state of religion at the time when Jeremiah was called to be a prophet we know from his contemporary Zephaniah, as well as from himself. The message of
the prophet Zephaniah centres in a single theme, the Day of
Yahweh. 'That day is a day of wrath, a day of trouble and
distress, a day of wasteness and desolation, a day of darkness
and gloominess, a day of clouds and thick darkness, a day of
the trumpet and alarm, against the fortified cities, and against
the high battlements' (i. 15, 16). It was the message which
Thomas of Celano echoed in the great mediæval Latin hymn,
'Dies irae, dies illa, solvet saeclum in favilla.' What language
could deserve to be coupled with the Hebrew for its sonorous
solemnity so well as the Latin—the great sister tongue of
worship?

> 'Tuba mirum spargens sonum
> Per sepulchra regionum
> Coget omnes ante thronum.'

But the trumpet which the prophet heard was not the same
as that which rang in the monk's cell, calling all men before
the judgment seat of God. It was the trumpet of armed attack,
the Day of Yahweh brought about by an armed host at a
definite point in the world's history. The agent of Yahweh's
Day of Judgment varies with the different periods of history;
each prophet naturally makes his own application of the
common idea, which may go back to a traditional group of
conceptions of the national destiny, though the prophets lifted
the idea out of the realm of myth and superstition, and transformed it by a new moral and religious content. For the
eighth-century prophets, the 'Day' was to be ushered in by
the Assyrians. But in the latter part of the seventh century,
the power of Assyria was waning, notwithstanding the vigorous
struggle and the temporary success of Ashurbanipal (668-626)
in seeking to arrest the decline. In his closing years the

Scythians seemed likely to be the power of the future. From about 630 they descended from their home north of the Crimea and invaded the more civilized lands of Mesopotamia and Syria, advancing as far on the way to Egypt as Ashdod, though not turning aside to Jerusalem. They are not actually named in the prophecies of Zephaniah or his contemporary Jeremiah, but it is usually held that the Scythians were conceived by both as the military agents of the Day of Yahweh. That Day, as Zephaniah conceives it, is to eradicate the current idolatry and paganism. Yahweh prepares a sacrifice, in which the slaughtered victims are the wicked in Judah, the guests who partake of the feast apparently being the Scythians. The classes to be punished are chiefly three—the court so servile to foreign fashion in religion, the merchants who care for nothing but the wealth destined to be a spoil for the enemy, and the indifferent who say, ' Yahweh will not do good, neither will He do evil.' The words of Zephaniah thus supply a valuable cross-section of the religious life at Jerusalem a decade or so after Manasseh's death, and some six years before the great reforming movement of Josiah :

'From this place I will cut off Baal to the last remnant, and the name of the idol-priests with the priests;
And those worshipping upon the roofs to the host of heaven;
And those worshipping who swear by Yahweh and who swear by Milcom;
And those who withdraw from following Yahweh;
Even those who have not sought Yahweh, and have not enquired of Him ' (i. 4-6).

This, then, was the spectacle which met the fresh eyes of the young man of Anathoth, both in his own village, less than four miles north-east of Jerusalem, and in the streets of that city itself. Well might he shrink from the call of God when it summoned him to challenge these vested interests, and denounce even the official religion of his day. He was no Amos, stern and uncompromising in temperament, no Amos of the desert, standing detached from the common ways of men, sent to the northern kingdom to proclaim the Day of Yahweh against personal strangers. He was more like Hosea in emotional temperament, affectionate and warm-hearted, loving men and the simple humanities of life, and, like Hosea, called to testify amongst his own people. He shrank from the call, not only because of his youthfulness, but surely because some deep instinct of the heart told him that he was the last man fitted for such a work. As he looked across the falling landscape eastwards from Anathoth to the distant hills of Gilead across the Jordan Valley, he must have foreseen the day when he would cry, 'Oh that I had in the wilderness a lodging-place of wayfaring men; that I might leave my people and go from them!' (ix. 2). But before we trace this inner struggle which gives so pathetic and so impressive a character to the prophetic activity of Jeremiah, we must realize the outer circumstances and events of his life, the outer and visible cross he had to bear.

There are five landmarks in that life, and his prophetic ministry was fulfilled under five kings of Judah, though the five landmarks do not correspond in time with the reigns of the five kings. The five kings are Josiah, Jehoahaz, Jehoiakim, Jehoiachin, and Zedekiah—but the reigns of the second and the fourth, Jehoahaz and Jehoiachin, were passing episodes, since they were limited to three months each. Virtually, therefore, the five kings become three—Josiah, the young and devout enthusiast, for whom to hear was to obey, who went to battle at Megiddo in loyal confidence in Yahweh, and was brought back dead in his chariot, not yet forty years of age; Jehoiakim, who rends the roll that his father would have reverenced, oppresses his people to meet the cost of his extravagance, and, with an ending to his life that seems not less undeserved than his father's, dies in peace, just in time to escape from the wrath of the Babylonians; Zedekiah, his brother, weak and vacillating, no leader either for good or ill, but swept into the whirlpool of rebellion by stronger men, to pay for his broken oath of allegiance by the worst fate of the three—for the last sight granted to his eyes before he was blinded was the murder of his sons. So they stand before us, clearly enough, in those days of the decline and fall of

Judah, and all that now remains of their regal activity is the part that each played in the life-story of the prophet of Anathoth.

The five landmarks in the life of Jeremiah are first, his call in 626, when Josiah was twenty-one, and the future prophet could have been little, if any, older; second, the Deuteronomic Reformation carried through by Josiah five years later in 621, though the prophet's relation to it is not so clear as we could wish; third, his challenge to Jehoiakim through the roll of Baruch in 604; fourth, his policy and sufferings during the siege of Jerusalem by the Babylonians, 588-586; fifth and last, his deportation to Egypt by some of his own countrymen. Here again, the five may be reduced to three, for the reformation of Josiah is rather an incident of Jeremiah's times than an event of his life, and the writing of the roll is important for the history of the book rather than of the man. Jeremiah, then, stands before us as the man first called to prophesy in 626 in the days of his youth, then, a generation after, called to suffer shame and peril in what should have been an honoured middle-age, and finally forced into exile in an alien land by men whose attitude and conduct were to him the sharpest reminder that he had spent his strength for nought and in vain. We need not speculate as to whether he met with violent death at their hands, as legend says; if so, that would have been a welcome end to the protracted martyrdom of his whole life. Isaiah had finished his career, so far as it is known to us, with a great victory, the deliverance of Jerusalem from Sennacherib, which his faith had so calmly and confidently anticipated. Jeremiah passes from our vision not less vindicated by the course of events, but vindicated by the destruction of the city he loved. As we fill in some of the details of his story we shall realize that his doing was chiefly in being, that the truth he brought was wrung out of life, and that his destiny was a passion, the bearing of a cross.

We have seen that Jeremiah's call to prophesy, like that of his contemporary, Zephaniah, had for its immediate occasion the advance of the Scythians into Assyrian territories, and that they came as far as Syria on their way to Egypt. Both these prophets see the hand of Yahweh in the restless encroachments

of these barbarians. This is the way in which Jeremiah pictures
their advance (iv. 5-9):

'Declare ye in Judah, and in Jerusalem publish it; and
say, "Blow ye the horn in the land": cry aloud and say,
"Assemble yourselves, and let us go into the fortified cities."
Lift up a way-mark toward Zion; bring your households into
safety, stay not: for evil am I bringing from the north, and
a great destruction. A lion is gone up from his thicket;
and a destroyer of nations is on his way, he is gone forth
from his place: to make thy land a desolation and that thy
cities be laid waste, without inhabitant. For this, gird you
with sackcloth, wail and howl: for the fierce anger of
Yahweh is not turned back from us.'

In the light of these events, we can understand the two
visions attached to the narrative of his call, with which his
prophetic experience begins (i. 11 f.). He sees the branch of
an almond-tree (shākēd), for which the Hebrew name is
'waker' or 'watcher', because it wakes to blossom as early
as February; the name suggests to him the waker or watcher
(shokēd), God, who slumbers not nor sleeps, but proceeds to
Judgment. Then he sees a boiling caldron, underneath which
is a fire fed from the northern side; it suggests to him the un-
happy lot of Judah, under whom the flames are kindled by
an enemy from the north.

Five years after the prophet's call, the nation of Judah was
brought under the influence of that 'Deuteronomic' party of
reform which had been created by the work of the eighth-
century prophets. Perhaps from the disciples whom Isaiah
had gathered round him, there had grown up a party of men,
under the long reign of Manasseh with all its paganism, who
were unable to obtain a hearing, but none the less prepared
for the dawn of a brighter day. The special form of their
activity was to draft in the prophetic spirit a programme of
national reformation. Their aim was to suppress all worship
not offered to Yahweh, and to clarify that which bore His
name. The means they adopted were to concentrate all
worship at the one temple of Jerusalem, where it could be

rigorously watched. Such proposals naturally gained the co-operation of the priests at Jerusalem, whose status was to become exclusive under the new régime. Other features of the movement were a strong insistence on social morality, more especially on justice and humanity towards the defence-less classes of the community, the plea for love to Yahweh as the only adequate fulfilling of the law, the moral interpretation of both past history and present Providence. All these features, it can be seen, are directly derived from the teaching of Amos and Hosea, Isaiah and Micah, and especially from Hosea so far as the religious spirit is concerned. But just as these prophets thought of themselves as recalling their people to forgotten principles rather than as leading them forward to new heights, so their disciples, the prophetic reformers, felt that they stood for the true and original worship of Yahweh. Consequently, they expressed their ideals in the form of legislation and ex-hortation, placed in the mouth of Moses, the traditional law-giver of the tribes of Israel. Thus was written the document now forming the nucleus of our Book of Deuteronomy. But the opportunity for promulgating it did not come until the dark days of Manasseh had passed away, and the stars in their courses no longer fought for their Assyrian worshippers. The reformation carried through by Josiah on the basis of this document owed its opportunity, therefore to the same political changes which mediated the call of contemporary prophets, including Jeremiah.

What was the attitude of Jeremiah to this movement? On general grounds we should expect it to have had his full sym-pathy, for it aimed at the ends dear to him, even if it failed, both in method and in ultimate result, to go as far as he wanted to take men. All practical reforms are of the nature of a compromise; if they were not, they would not be practical. Jeremiah's name is not, indeed, mentioned in the account of the reformation, but in that there is nothing surprising. He may have been discredited by the diversion of the Scythian invasion (cf. xvii. 15); again, he was a young man, probably little known; he was not a man to seek notoriety; and there is always in Hebrew prophecy an incalculable element, an element responsible for either speech or silence where we might have expected the opposite. According to one passage in the present Book of Jeremiah, the prophet was actually commissioned to go about as a sort of itinerant preacher of the reformation (xi. 6): 'Proclaim all these words in the cities of Judah, and in the streets of Jerusalem, saying, "Hear ye the words of this covenant, and do them."' But whatever was the degree of the prophet's participation, there can be no doubt as to his disappointment with the outcome of the movement. A passage that follows the words just quoted implies the failure of the reform: 'they are turned back'. The failure was brought home to the people by the tragic end of Josiah on the battlefield of Megiddo; for who had a better right than he to look for the active help and protection of Yahweh? There must have followed a great revulsion of feeling, even if the externalism of the devotion to the one sanctuary had not already shown its lack of spirituality. Jeremiah may even be criticizing the Deuteronomic Code when he says:

'How do ye say, "We are wise, and the law of Yahweh is with us?" But surely, behold, the false pen of the scribes hath wrought falsely' (viii. 8).

At any rate, Jeremiah must have been getting out of touch with contemporary forms of religious zeal, even of the re-formed order, in the later years of Josiah's reign, during which his prophetic voice is silent. It is not until a new period of storm and stress is introduced by the death of Josiah and the change of kings that he comes forward again, and then it is to condemn in plainest terms the folly of dependence on the mere possession of the temple, which Deuteronomy had done so much to emphasize.

One experience of the prophet, itself prophetic of what was to be true of his life as a whole, may belong to the time of the Deuteronomic Reformation, and to Jeremiah's possible participation in it. This was a plot of the men of Anathoth, his native place, against his life. We can easily believe that an enthusiastic advocacy of the destruction of the local high-place and its familiar worship, whether or not in conjunction with the new emphasis on the Jerusalem temple, would stir

K

up strong local enmities and violence. For all we know, this opposition may have been aroused by some particular utterance (like that of the men of Nazareth to *their* young Prophet), making them cry, 'Thou shalt not prophesy in the name of Yahweh, that thou die not by our hand.' It would be accentuated by the fact that the speaker himself was 'of the priests that were in Anathoth' (i. 1), and that the priestly descendants of Abiathar in Anathoth would strongly resent a movement which set them aside for ever in favour of the Zadokite priests of Jerusalem. The reference to this plot is found in the same chapter as that which speaks of the Deuteronomic Reformation, a fact which so far confirms our interpretation of it:

> 'But Yahweh made me know, and I knew;
>   Then did He shew me their deeds;
> Whilst I was like a gentle lamb
>   That is led to the slaughter;
> I knew not it was against me
>   That they schemed their schemes:—
> "Let us spoil the tree in its sap,
> Cut him off from the land of the living,
> That his name be remembered no more"' (xi. 18, 19).

This local and perhaps professional enmity towards the prophet was exhibited even by the members of Jeremiah's own family (xii. 6):

> 'For even thy brethren and the house of thy father, even *they* have dealt treacherously with thee, even they have cried aloud after thee: believe them not, when they speak fair words unto thee.'

This is the first account we have of the isolation and peril in which Jeremiah was to live, and it will be seen that it belongs to the earliest years of his work. In the next period, under Jehoiakim, the arena is a larger one—Jerusalem instead of Anathoth, the Temple instead of the high-place of the village, priests and people of the city instead of villagers and kinsmen.

It was one thing to denounce the worship of a village high-place with all the prestige of a national movement behind the speaker, it was quite another to attack the worship of that Temple which the movement had done so much to exalt. Perhaps the consciousness of such greater tasks ahead was present already in the earlier days, for a message of Yahweh to the prophet then had been:

'If thou hast run with the footmen, and they have wearied thee, then how canst thou contend with horses? and if in a land of peace thou dost flee, then how wilt thou do in the jungle of Jordan?' (xii. 5).

Whatever the prophet's misgivings had been or still were, he met the new demands of Jehoiakim's reign with an un-daunted front. At the beginning of that reign he steps into a new prominence with the 'Temple Sermon', calling men away from reliance on the outward means of grace, and narrowly escaping with his life, as we have already learnt from the biographical narrative of Baruch. Four years later, after the battle of Carchemish, when the Egyptians had been so definitely defeated by the new power of the Babylonians, he challenged the king and his policy by not less definitely declaring that God was making the Babylonians the instruments of His vengeance upon Jerusalem, as again we have heard from Baruch. This time he escaped death only by going into hiding. At some time between these two incidents he had used the symbolism of an earthenware flask, publicly broken, to declare the breaking up of the city, because of its alien worship, its injustice, its sacrifice of children by fire. He had said all this first to a representative group overlooking the valley of Hinnom; even that defiled valley will have to be used for burials, he says, so many will be the deaths. He then went to the Temple courts, and spoke to the same effect more publicly, with the result that the chief officer of the Temple had him beaten and put in the stocks (xix. 1-xx. 6). His attitude to Jehoiakim as a king is sufficiently indicated in the short oracle in which he contrasted him with his father, Josiah:

'Woe to him who builds his house with unrighteousness,
    And his chambers with injustice!
Who employs his neighbour for nothing,
    And does not give him his pay:
Who says, "I will build me a spacious house,
    And roomy chambers";
Windows for it he carves out,
    Panelling with cedar, painting with vermilion.

Art thou king by competing in cedar?
Did not thy father eat and drink,
    Doing justice and righteousness in prosperity?
He judged the cause of the needy and poor,
    Then did he prosper;
Was not this to know me?
    —saith Yahweh.

But thine eyes and thy purpose
    Are on naught but thy gain,
On the shedding of innocent blood,
    On oppression and crushing deeds' (xxii. 13-17).

If Jeremiah's prophecy about this king's miserable end
(xxxvi. 30) was not actually fulfilled, his general message
received full vindication in 597, when the city had to surrender
to Nebuchadrezzar, as a result of Jehoiakim's rebellion against
him, and his son and brief successor Jehoiachin, was carried
a prisoner into Babylon. Many of the upper classes and more
efficient elements of the nation, though not imprisoned, were
deported, thus becoming the first of the Babylonian exiles.

It must have been, then, with a new prestige that Jeremiah
entered on the next period of his life, under Zedekiah, whom
Nebuchadrezzar placed at the head of the depleted and much
weakened state. The prophet was a person of consequence,
however unpopular, as we see from the frequent resort of the
weak king to him for counsel. This is seen in particular with
reference to the abortive conspiracy of 594, through which a
number of Syrian states, whose representatives gathered at
Jerusalem, planned to throw off the yoke of Babylon. By the

symbolism of a yoke upon his own neck, and by his spoken word, Jeremiah exerted himself, not in vain, against this disastrous policy, and for some years Jerusalem enjoyed peace. But in 588 the final rebellion did break out, and the long siege of Jerusalem by the Babylonians began, to end in 586 with the capture of the city and the final downfall of the Jewish State. Here Baruch's biography of the prophet is full and detailed, and the siege becomes a dramatic background to his personal fortunes. Because of his repeated testimony that the siege could end in but one way, the king was compelled to imprison him (xxxii. 3, xxxiii. 1). During the interval when the siege was raised, owing to the Egyptians, Jeremiah was leaving the city to visit his native place when he was arrested on the charge, not unnatural, of deserting to the enemy (xxxvii. 13). But for a secret interview with the king, and an appeal to him, Jeremiah would have been left to die in prison. According to another narrative (which may be either a duplicate version or a distinct incident), Jeremiah was flung into a muddy pit at the instigation of the enraged leaders, who quite rightly felt that Jeremiah's influence and prophecies were weakening the city's spirit of resistance. It was a foreigner, an Ethiopian, an officer of the king, who was now the means of saving him; with the king's consent, and with considerable physical difficulty, Jeremiah was drawn up from the pit, and put in the court of the guard (xxxviii.).

Jeremiah's sufferings were not over when the city was captured by the Babylonians, though he had nothing to fear from *them*. They appointed a governor of Jewish origin to the oversight of those whom they did not deport to Babylon, and Jeremiah was allowed to remain with him. Gedaliah, the governor, might have established a permanent Jewish community on a peaceful basis, had he not been treacherously murdered. As it was, the band of men who had gathered round him thought it safest to migrate to Egypt, where there had been Jewish settlements for a long time. Jeremiah was asked for an oracle of Yahweh as to this plan, which shows the place he held in men's eyes; but when at length he was able to give one, counselling stay in Palestine they disregarded the guidance they had sought, and carried Baruch and Jeremiah with them into Egypt. We hear him there, for the last time, rebuking the heathenism which had mingled with the true religion of Yahweh's worshippers, and had mingled all the more because it seemed to them that the worship of Yahweh alone had disastrously failed them. According to a late tradition, Jeremiah was stoned to death by his own countrymen.

Even when considered only from an outer point of view, it is plain that there is no life in the Old Testament which more closely resembles the life of our Lord. Jeremiah was prepared for his work in a village home, but the time came when Anathoth ceased to be a home for him as did Nazareth for Jesus, and his friends must often have said of him, as was said of Jesus, 'He is beside himself.' The words and deeds of both were jealously watched by plotting rivals (xviii. 18). The externalism of the Temple worship, the worldliness and immorality of those who were chiefly responsible for it, crucified his spirit, as they did that of Jesus. There is a very real parallel between the prophet of Anathoth standing at the Temple gate to denounce the futility of confidence in empty forms, and the prophet of Nazareth overthrowing the tables of the money-changers within it, whilst he quoted this prophet's own words, 'Ye have made it a den of robbers.' Those words brought Jeremiah to the very verge of death as they brought Jesus beyond it. But for both the son of man and the Son of God the sorest pain was not scourging or death, but that agony of spirit which sees the tragic drift of those well loved, whilst it is powerless to arrest their course. Both were lovers of men, and the lovers of men will never enjoy denouncing them. Jeremiah and Jesus both wept over Jerusalem. So there were good grounds for those who in our Lord's time identified Him with the prophet of Anathoth, come back to earth, and there is peculiar congruity in the fact that the figure of the Lamb of God, which has become the rightful name of Jesus, historically and primarily belongs to this forerunner of His, who said of *himself*, with perfect truth, that he was like a lamb led to the slaughter. There is a point, of course, at which the resemblance ceases. Jesus did not say of those who crucified Him, 'Pardon Thou not their iniquities,' and

Jeremiah never said of his persecutors, 'Father, forgive them, for they know not what they do.' Yet the prophet carried a cross before Christ, and carried it, more than any other in the Old Testament, in the spirit of Christ.

If we attentively consider the successive phases of Jeremiah's life, as they have been briefly outlined, we shall see both the underlying unity of aim and purpose which gives consistency to that life, and also the persistency of opposition which that aim and purpose evoked. In the early days at Anathoth, he disentangled himself from family, professional and local ties to preach a purer worship and a truer covenant with God. In the middle phase under Jehoiakim, he advanced into a larger arena to attack the Temple itself, when it was made the substitute for an inward religion, a personal relation to God. In the final phase of Zedekiah, he breaks loose from all national ties, and accepts the destruction of the nation, without the thought of any 'righteous remnant' to preserve its continuity, such as Isaiah had. He is able to make this thorough break with one entanglement after another, just because he has gone so far in the realization of what personal religion, in the last resort, must mean. Our study of that inner consciousness comes later, but its presence must be noted here, as the positive strength of Jeremiah's teaching, underneath so much that seems simply negative.

A similar line of thought will show us why Jeremiah had to encounter so much unpopularity and suffering. In one sense, all the pre-exilic prophets of Israel were unpopular, for they strongly condemned the social life and religious practices of their contemporaries and foretold the just penalty in political misfortune and national disaster. So long as Jeremiah simply pointed to the Scythian and the Babylonian, saying, 'Behold the agents of Yahweh!' he was saying no more than Amos and Hosea and Isaiah and Micah had said before him about the Assyrian. But Jeremiah went further. In the last siege, when his attitude becomes clearest to us, as perhaps it then became clearest to himself, he counselled men to go forth to the enemy and welcome the destruction of the nation—to bear the cross not, like Simon of Cyrene, because they had to, but voluntarily, as true disciples, like the sons of Simon.

He was technically guilty of high treason, for he urged surrender to the enemy whilst their besieging army lay round
the walls of Jerusalem, and he urged it, not as a matter of
public policy and common action only, but as something to
be commended to the individual, quite regardless of the State.
This is his definite advice in Yahweh's name to Zedekiah, who
sought his counsel: ' If thou goest forth unto the king of Babylon's princes, then thou shalt live, and this city will not be
burned with fire . . . but if thou goest not forth to the king
of Babylon's princes, then will this city be given into the hand
of the Chaldeans and they will burn it with fire, and *thou* wilt
not escape out of their hand' (xxxvii. 17, 18). To the people
generally, Jeremiah declared that the defence of the city was
hopeless, and individual surrender to the enemy was the only
chance of life:

> ' Thus said Yahweh, He that abideth in this city shall die
> by the sword, by the famine and by the pestilence: but he
> that goeth forth to the Chaldeans shall live, and his life shall
> be his booty, and he shall live. Thus saith Yahweh, This
> city shall surely be given into the hand of the king of
> Babylon's army, and he shall capture it' (xxxviii. 2, 3).

Jeremiah's advice was not the product of cowardly and
calculating expediency, nor was it, as it has sometimes been
called, ' pacifism '. We might as well call his recognition of
the use God is making of the Babylonian army ' militarism ' as
call his attitude to surrender ' pacifism '. It is simply the
definite application of his faith in Yahweh's control of human
affairs. Long before the siege began, he had proclaimed that
Yahweh had temporarily committed all power into the hands
of Nebuchadrezzar (xxvii. 5 f.). In reality, Jeremiah's declaration that the Babylonians would capture Jerusalem was just as
patriotic as Isaiah's that the Assyrians would not. Jeremiah
has seen the disloyalty to Yahweh of Mannasseh's reign, the
failure of legislative reform to change the heart of a people,
the oppressive tyranny of Jehoiakim, the callous indifference
of Zedekiah to his pledged word—and all this in a people
miraculously spared, when its northern sister had been carried

into captivity. Indeed, the cup of Yahweh's wrath was filled to the brim (xxv. 15 f.).

We have also to remember that though Jeremiah saw no present continuity of the nation, only the continuity of personal religion in the individual, he did look beyond present disaster and national destruction to a future which Yahweh would make prosperous. He expressed his faith dramatically through his deliberate purchase of a field at Ana-thoth with all legal formalities, a field on which the besiegers were at that moment encamped. His act was explicitly declared to be a token that 'Houses and fields and vineyards shall yet again be bought in this land' (xxxii. 15)—an act like that of the Roman who bought at undiminished price the field on which Hannibal was encamped with his army (Livy, xxvi. 11). Jeremiah foretold that Yahweh would bring Judah back to her land after seventy years—a round number, meaning two or three generations (xxix. 10). He was as sure as his younger contemporary, Ezekiel, that the future lay, not with those left in Judah, the dregs of a nation, but with the exiles of Babylon, as indeed it did.

The full significance of Jeremiah's passion and cross can be considered only when we have examined the record of his inner experience, which is the great glory of his legacy to us. But one clear truth may be placed alongside the thoughts which arise in us when we think of such sorrows as his accompanying the loyal service of God. The cross without is inevitable for the full realization of the cross within. If, as the Christian faith proclaims, the deepest experience of God is to be found only through the fellowship of the cross, that fellowship must be no sentimental ideal, no esoteric and hidden desire, but something worked out amid the realities of life. Let us recall again those familiar words of Milton, which can never be quoted too often by those who would summon men to the realities of personal religion: 'I cannot praise a fugitive and cloistered virtue, unexercised and unbreathed, that never sallies out and sees her adversary, but slinks out of the race, where that immortal garland is to be run for, not without dust and heat.'

THE CROSS WITHIN

LORD MORLEY, in his study of Oliver Cromwell, speaks of his hero's speeches as 'not coherent, not smooth, not always even intelligible, but with a strain of high-hearted fervour in them that pierces through rugged and uncouth forms . . . still impressive by their labouring sincerity, by the weight of their topics, and by that which is the true force of all oratory worth talking about, the momentum of the speaker's history, personality, and purpose' (p. 390). In many things, Cromwell and Jeremiah are in strong contrast, but the same truth holds of their utterances. It is the momentum of Jeremiah's personality that we have now to realize, so as to supplement, or rather to explain, the momentum of his history already reviewed. We are singularly fortunate in being able to do this in a most intimate way. Scattered through the earlier part of the Book of Jeremiah there are a number of autobiographical poems, poems, which can hardly have been any part of his public message, even though they were subsequently incorporated in Baruch's roll. It is probably to Baruch that we owe the preservation of this incomparable material for understanding Jeremiah's inner life. There is nothing like it in the Old Testament, no similar revelation of any other figure of Old Testament history. The prophet might have said of these poems what another poet of our own time, Francis Thompson, has said of his, 'often verse written as I write it is nothing less than a confessional far more intimate than the sacerdotal one' (*Life*, p. 103). How difficult it is to achieve success in a direct autobiography we know from the many attempts and the few classics. Amiel's *Journal* is one of the few, partly because it was not written for publication, and Amiel himself speaks of the impossibility of an adequate revelation of the inner self, in terms that are singularly appropriate to Jeremiah :

'For the great things of life we are always alone, and our true history is hardly ever deciphered by others. The greater part of this drama is a monologue, or rather an intimate debate between God, our consciousness and ourselves. Tears, griefs, prostrations, deceptions, bruisings, evil and good thoughts, decisions, uncertainties, deliberations— all that is our secret. Almost all of it is incommunicable, not to be transmitted, even when we wish to speak of it, even when we write it' (Oct. 27th, 1856).

Perhaps Jeremiah achieved the impossible by forgetting himself in his poetic art, by coming, like many a poet and preacher, to think of his inner life as no longer his own, but something laid on the altar of God. These short poems are full of historical interest, because they reveal so much of the true nature of the prophetic consciousness. But they have a still greater significance for religious experience. They blaze new pathways through the trackless forests where men have sought for God. They show us how religious experience may itself become sacramental. They become windows through which we are allowed to look into a spiritual temple, and to say, reverently, of what we see, 'Behold, he prayeth!'

We cannot date these confessional lyrics with any exactitude, nor can we be sure that the order in which they are now preserved represents the order of their occasions. But it is natural to suppose that they belong rather to the reign of Josiah than to that of later kings, and represent the spiritual struggle in the prophet's heart before he had committed himself to his more public ministry under Jehoiakim. That ministry was the result of the inner victory of faith in the previous struggle, and the records show us how much it cost the man. We may arrange them in three groups, viz., those in which the prophet's sense of loneliness is the dominating thought, those which show how his suffering was accentuated by intense sympathy with the people against whom he was called to testify, and those which show us his divided heart and the divine compulsion. The best preface is the prophet's account of his call, which has already been quoted:

'Yahweh said to me: —
Before I shaped thee unborn I knew thee,
Before thou camest forth from the womb I conse-
    crated thee,
For a prophet to the nations have I given thee.'

As Duhm finely says, Jeremiah feels himself to have been
'a thought of God', before the divine hands shaped his limbs
according to the pattern of that thought. It must be remembered that the body, not the soul, is the essential personality
for Hebrew psychology; man is an animated body, not an
incarnated soul as with the Greeks. The prophet is not only
youthful, but altogether lacking in self-confidence, and he cries
'Ah, Lord Yahweh, I do not know how to speak, for I am
young.' Then comes the divine answer, 'Do not say, I am
(too) young; for to whomsoever I shall send thee thou shalt
go, and whatsoever I shall command thee thou shalt speak.
Fear not because of them, for with thee am I to deliver thee,
saith Yahweh.' Then he experiences that touch of God's hand
upon his mouth that claims it as a divine instrument. That
experience takes us to the heart of both the weakness and the
strength of Jeremiah, as will be seen in the poems, when we
read them. He never loses the sense of his own insufficiency,
but again and again he is brought back to the sufficiency of
God. The centre of gravity is transferred from his own heart
to God's; the consciousness of dependence is this prophet's
strength to a unique degree. So it is that after the two visions
indicating his special mission, he hears the voice which says,
'I make thee this day a fortified city, and a bronze wall against
the whole land.' As Sir George Adam Smith points out, the
words 'imply that in himself Jeremiah was something different.
God does not speak thus to a man unless He sees that he
needs it. It was to his most impetuous and unstable disciple
that Christ said, *Thou art Peter, and on this rock will I build*'
(*Jeremiah*, p. 333). There is something in Jeremiah of that
strange conviction which religious men so often have, that
they are being used of God at their weakest point, and not
at their strongest. It is essentially the same experience as
that of the Apostle Paul, when he hears the words, 'My

grace is sufficient for thee; for power is made perfect in weakness.'

The sense of helplessness in the presence of the brute forces of life meets us in the poem that refers to the plot of the men of Anathoth against his life, which has already been quoted:

> 'But Yahweh made me know, and I knew;
>   Then did He shew me their deeds;
> Whilst I was like a gentle lamb
>   That is led to the slaughter;
> I knew not it was against me
>   That they schemed their schemes:—
> "Let us spoil the tree in its sap,
> Cut him off from the land of the living,
> That his name be remembered no more "' (xi. 18, 19).

Apparently through this experience, if we may judge from the context, the prophet was brought face to face with that long-debated problem of Israel, the prosperity of the wicked:

> 'Thou art in the right, O Yahweh,
>   When I bring my suit to Thee;
> Yet would I speak with thee of judgments.
>
> Why is the way of the wicked prosperous,
>   And all dealers in treachery at ease?
> Thou plantest them, they also take root,
>   They grow and bring forth fruit.
> Thou art (near) in their mouth,
>   But far away from their heart.
>
> But Thou, O Yahweh, dost know me,
>   Dost see me, testing my heart with Thee.
> Pull them out like sheep for the slaughter,
>   For a day of slaying devote them' (xii. 1-3).

That final imprecation comes with a shock to Christian susceptibilities, but we must take Jeremiah as we find him, and not forget his historical place in the history of revelation. His achievement in the realm of personal religion is realized only when we take full account of his limitations, from a Christian standpoint. Another poem describes a similar situation at some later stage of the prophet's life:

    ' " Come," they said, " let us scheme
        Schemes against Jeremiah,
    (For teaching shall not perish from priest,
        Nor counsel from sage, nor word from prophet,)
    Come, with the tongue let us smite him,
        Let us watch all his words."

    Watch Thou me, O Yahweh!
        And list to my uttered plea;
    Shall evil be requited for good,
        That a pit they have dug for my life?
    Remember my standing before Thee,
        To speak for their good,
        To turn thy rage from them. . . .

    But *Thou*, O Yahweh, dost know
        All their plans for my death.
    Cover not over their guilt,
        Blot not their sin from Thy sight.
    Let them lie overthrown before Thee,
        In the time of Thy anger deal with them '
                                (xviii. 18-20, 23).

    How it must have hurt Jeremiah in the most sensitive part of his nature when his prophectic message was doubted and openly scoffed at! Thrown back on himself by such an attitude, he found his comfort in reminding Yahweh that he had been a faithful, though unwilling messenger:

    ' Heal me, Yahweh, that I may be healed,
        Save me that I may be saved,
            For thou art my praise!

    Lo! *they* keep saying to me,
        " Where is the word of Yahweh?
            Pray, let it come! "

But *I* have not pressed Thee for evil,
   Nor longed for the day of disaster,
      Thou knowest.

What has come forth from my lips
   Is open before Thy face.

Be not a terror to me,
   My refuge, Thou, in the day of evil;
Let my pursuers be shamed, and not me!
   Let *them* be dismayed, and not me!
Bring the day of evil upon them;
   Destroy them with doubled destruction'

(xvii. 14-18).

The cardinal passage describing the prophet's loneliness is that in which he laments his birth, and reproaches Yahweh with his undeserved sufferings:

'Woe is me, my mother, that thou hast borne me,
   A man of contentious strife with all the world!
Neither lender nor borrower was I,
   Yet all of them curse me!
Speak, Lord, if I have not persisted
   With Thee for (the enemy's) good,
Interceding with Thee in the evil time,
   In the time of distress for the enemy. . . .

Thou knowest, Yahweh!
   Remember and care for me;
Take vengeance for me on my pursuers,
   Remove me not through thy patience (with them).

When I found Thy words, they were my food,
   To me thy words were a delight,
      The joy of my heart;
For Thy name has been called over me,
   O Yahweh, God of Hosts!

In the circle of the merry I sat not rejoicing,
　　Because of Thy hand I sat alone,
　　　For with wrath hast Thou filled me.
Why is my pain perpetual,
　　My wound sore, refusing to be healed?
Wilt Thou be to me like a lying stream,
　　Like waters that are not sure?' (xv. 10-18).

To this bitter cry of reproach comes the answer of Yahweh, of the greatest importance for the understanding of the prophetic consciousness, because it tells us that the message rested on what we call technically to-day a 'value-judgment', an acceptance of truth on the ground of its intrinsic character:

'If thou return, I will restore thee,
　　Before Me shalt thou stand:
If thou bring out the precious from the common,
　　Thou shalt be as my mouth.
They shall return to thee,
　　Thou shalt not return to them.
I will make thee to this people
　　An unscaled wall of bronze;
They will fight against thee, unable to overcome thee,
　　For with thee am I, to save and rescue thee;
I will rescue thee from the hand of the evil (man),
　　And redeem thee from the grasp of the terrible'
　　　　　　　　　　　　　　　　　　　(xv. 19-21).

The sense of isolation and loneliness which sprang from the prophetic mission of Jeremiah in relation to his times was itself accentuated by the second feature of these poems—the spiritual suffering which was his owing to his intense sympathy with the people over whom he must proclaim the judgment of God. This is seen from the earliest days, when he discerns the peril from the north:

'My heart. my heart! let me writhe!
　　O walls of my heart!

My heart is in tumult within;
  I cannot keep still,
For the sound of the horn do I hear,
  The blast of battle!

Crash upon crash it comes—
  For all the land is ravaged
Of a sudden my tent is ravaged
  In an instant my curtains.
How long must I see the standard,
  Hear the sound of the horn?' (iv. 19-21).

The striking vision which follows this outbreak, though not strictly one of the autobiographical poems, must be quoted here, because it enables us better to understand the prophet's anguish:

'I saw the earth—and behold! a chaos!
  The heavens—and their light was gone.
I saw the mountains—and behold! they trembled,
  And all the hills moved to and fro.
I saw—and behold! no man was there,
  And all the birds of heaven were flown.
I saw—and behold! the cornland was desert,
  And all its cities were pulled down,
    From before Yahweh, from before His fierce anger'
                                          (iv. 23-26).

The prophet is one with his people in their sorrows, however much these are well deserved:

'Without healing is my sorrow,
  My heart upon me is faint.
Hark! my people's cry of distress
  From a land that is far away: —
"Is Yahweh not in Zion?
  Is not her King there?
The harvest is over, the summer is ended,
  And we are not saved."

L

> For the breaking of my people am I broken,
>   Seized by horror, I mourn;
> Is there no balm in Gilead?
> Is there no healer there?
> Why then does it not come,
>   The healing of my people's wound?
>
> O that my head were waters,
>   And my eyes a fountain of tears!
> That day and night I might weep
>   Over the slain of my people ' (viii. 18-ix. 1).

Even so, the prophet's desire to intercede with Yahweh for his people was sternly checked by the divine command: ' As for thee, pray not for this people, nor lift up for them a ringing cry and prayer; and do not make intercession with Me, for I hear thee not' (vii. 16), a warning repeated more than once (xi. 14, xiv. 11).

From this point of view we can the better understand the prophet's divided heart, and the long-drawn-out conflict between the natural shrinking of his temperament, seen in his call, and reinforced by his natural sympathies, on the one hand, and on the other, the spectacle of the sin that called for punishment, and the consciousness that he was divinely commissioned to proclaim it, in Yahweh's name. As Skinner points out, ' The central interest of the " Confessions " is the struggle in Jeremiah's mind between fidelity to his prophetic commission and the natural feelings and impulses of his heart' (p. 210). The spiritual crown of thorns which the prophet wore is well indicated in a fine sentence of George Eliot, in which she speaks of ' that thorn-pressure which must come with the crowning of the sorrowful better, suffering because of the worst.' It was not that the element in his nature which made him struggle against his office was in itself wrong; on the contrary, it was natural that with such a temperament he should shrink from the task, and right that he should feel the sorrow of a great sympathy with those whose coming suffering he must proclaim. But for him there was a higher duty—obedience, and an obedience which of necessity was crowned with thorns:

'Of the wrath of Yahweh am I full,
  Tired of restraining it;
"Pour it out on the child in the street,
  On the group of young men together;
For man and wife shall be taken,
  The old with the full of days
And their houses shall pass to others,
  Fields and wives together"' (vi. 11, 12).

But the chief passage telling of the sorrows of the divine
compulsion is that in the twentieth chapter, which ranks with
that in the fifteenth as of primary importance for our knowledge of Jeremiah's inner life (7-12):

'Thou hast deceived me, Yahweh; and I was
    deceived:
  Thou wast stronger than I and didst prevail;
I became a laughing-stock all the day,
  All men mock me.

Whenever I speak I am derided;
  "Violence" and "ravage" I proclaim;
For Yahweh's word has become my reproach,
  My derision all the day.

When I say, "I will not recall Him,
  I will speak no more in His name,"
In my heart is a burning fire,
  Enclosed in my bones.
I am weary with holding it in,
  I am not able (to do it).

For I hear the whisper of many:
  "Denounce! Yes, let us denounce him!
All ye his intimate friends,
  Watch ye his stumbling;
He may haply be deceived, and we prevail,
  Taking vengeance upon him."

But Yahweh is with me, mighty and terrible,
    Therefore my pursuers shall stumble, and not
        prevail!
Utterly shamed for their unwisdom,
    With endless, unforgotten, disgrace.

But Yahweh of hosts, Thou righteous Tester!
    Who seest emotions and will;
Let me see Thy vengeance upon them,
    For on Thee have I rolled my cause.' (xx. 7-12).

This revealing poem is followed by another which, in all
probability, has inspired the opening poem of the Book of Job
(c. iii.; in which Job, after the following Jeremianic pattern,
curses his birth because of his sorrows):

'Curs'd be the day when I was born,
    The day when my mother bore me—
        Let it have no blessing!
Curs'd be the man who announced to my father
    "A man-child is born!" making him glad.

Let that day be like the cities
    That Yahweh o'erthrew without pity;
Let it hear a cry in the morning,
    A shout at the noontide;
Because it slew me not at the womb,
    That my mother had been my grave,
        And her womb with child for ever.

Why then came I forth from the womb,
    To see trouble and sorrow,
        That my days be wasted with shame?' (xx. 14-18).

It may help us to realize the essential nature of the struggle
in the prophet's divided heart to remember that this curse on
the prophet's pre-natal existence is really a curse on the divine
thought which shaped him then and there for this destiny.

Put like that, it seems an appalling blasphemy; yet it is better to put things in their primitive truth than to wrap them up and conceal the real issue. The moral and spiritual struggle always is between some thought of God concerning us, and that rival thought of ourselves which challenges His. From such a conflict alone is the prize of high and precious truth wrested, or to change the figure for what is a better one, the truth would not be born without these travail-pangs. Here is the point of the great word of Yahweh to the prophet, 'If pure thoughts thou utter, unmixed with base, Thou shalt be as My Mouth' (xv. 19). There could hardly be a better commentary on, or parallel with, this inner experience of a poet-prophet than the verses which a modern poet, Alfred Noyes, has devoted to the same theme:

'There is a Master in my heart
    To whom, though oft against my will,
I bring the songs I sing apart
    And strive to think that they fulfil
His silent law, within my heart.

But He is blind to my desires,
    And deaf to all that I would plead:
He tests my truth at purer fires
    And shames my purple with His need.
He claims my deeds, not my desires.

And often, when my comrades praise,
    I sadden, for He turns from me.
But, sometimes, when they blame, I raise
    Mine eyes to His, and in them see
A tenderness too deep for praise.

He is not to be bought with gold,
    Or lured by thornless crowns of fame;
But when some rebel thought hath sold
    Him to dishonour and to shame,
And my heart's Pilate cries "Behold,"

" Behold the Man," I know Him then;
  And all those wild thronged clamours die
In my heart's judgment-hall again,
  Or if it ring with " Crucify ! "
Some few are faithful even then.

Some few sad thoughts,—one bears His cross,
  To that dark Calvary of my pride;
One stands far off and mourns His loss,
  And one poor thief on either side
Hangs on his own unworthy cross.

And one—O, truth in ancient guise!—
  Rails, and one bids him cease alway,
And the God turns His hungering eyes
  On that poor thought with " Thou, this day,
Shalt sing, shalt sing, in Paradise." [1]

We are taught, therefore, in these poems of Jeremiah's inner
life, to regard prophetic truth as no bolt from the blue, but
as something with a psychological history, which can in no
small degree be traced, though there is a point at which our
powers of analysis necessarily fail, a point at which the ultimate contact of human personality with the divine removes
itself from our enquiry. We can see that the words and deeds
of Jeremiah as a prophet were partly temperamental and
instinctive, partly due to intelligent and reflective consideration
of the life about him, and partly the will of a power not himself, the personality of God in contact with his own, com-
pelling him to deliver a message, even against his own will.
That he was subject to abnormal experiences, as we should
regard them, there can be little doubt—visions, auditions,
pressures, that did not come through the familiar channels of
sight and hearing and touch, though to him they would seem
to do so. Words that seem to us the exaggerated language of
poetry may often express what was for him a very literal truth.
It is so when he speaks of his physical condition, as he regards
the profanity of prophet and priest :

[1] ' The Inner Passion,' *Collected Poems*, iii., pp. 365-6, quoted by kind permission of the author and the publishers, Messrs. William Blackwood & Sons.

'Broken is my heart within me,
   All my bones are strengthless.
I am like a drunken man,
   Like one overcome by wine,
Before Yahweh and His holy words' (xxiii. 9).

There we have just the same phenomena as are recorded of the day of Pentecost, when onlookers say of those under the influence of the Spirit, 'They are filled with new wine.' We know how Jeremiah was regarded by sober officials of his day. Shemaiah wrote to the officers of the Temple, reminding them that it was their duty in regard to every man that was mad, and made himself a prophet, to put him in the stocks and shackles, and asking why this had not been done to Jeremiah (xxix. 26, 27; it had been done at an earlier date, xx. 2). In plain words, the conduct even of a Jeremiah could be represented as that of a man out of his mind, just as Elisha's prophetic messenger to Jehu is called by the officers of his staff, 'this mad fellow' (2 Kings ix. 11). There was probably no psychological test by which true prophets could have been distinguished from false. But this traditional accompaniment of the prophetic consciousness has long since ceased to be the chief element, which is the sub-conscious and the conscious use of all moral and spiritual powers, under the divine influence and in clear relation to the life of the times. Our present study shows us what it meant at its highest, for it is at its highest in the person of Jeremiah. His experience is that of a dialogue with God, in which he fully maintains his own individual consciousness, and argues with God as with a fellow-man. Doubtless the prophet is unconscious of the degree to which the words of both speakers in the debate are his own, the degree to which God is speaking man's language, even when His will is asserting itself against that of the prophet. Sometimes, even in our own experience, some word or words will take shape in our consciousness and assert themselves with an objective quality as not our own thought at all. In a dream, for example, when our ordinary control of consciousness is suspended, we may distinctly hear such words spoken as by another, and some have had such experiences in waking life.

Much more was it so in those days of a different psychology, and an attitude less checked by intellectual inhibitions. In one sense, all that a prophet could give was his own, even when he spoke in the name of Yahweh. But this is simply to say that whatever incommunicable experience of God was the prophet's, it had to be translated into intelligible speech before it could become of use to others. The very condition of such experience is an ethical conflict of the kind we have seen in the poems, for God must reveal Himself as something higher, as against our lower, if He is to be recognizable. It has been said that one of the most important truths about the moral life is its 'law of tension'—that progress is dependent on the very strain and stress which it is so hard to endure, which is another way of saying that revelation is always the other side of discovery. Up to a given point, which we may call the breaking-point, the harder we are strained, the more the possibility of moral and spiritual gain. We are apt to forget this in the instance of men of high moral and spiritual attainment; as we look up to their higher plane, it does not seem that 'they wrestled hard as we do now, with sins and doubts and fears.' This is one reason why Jeremiah's autobiographic record is so valuable. Here is one of the admitted princes of the spirit— and here is a man who has so revealed himself to us that we can see how acute the tension was, and how often it must have seemed to him that the breaking-point was reached. The working of the law of tension demands that it be our own selves that feel the strain, and, therefore, the occasion must arise naturally and inevitably from that which we are, and from that in which we are. Sometimes there may seem to be a malignant choice at work, intimate with our hidden weaknesses, and putting on the strain just where it is most unfair. That was, as we have seen, peculiarly true for Jeremiah. Joseph Conrad, in his Lord Jim, reminds us that every honest man would confess to there being a point—for the best of us —when he would let go everything. Since God alone can know where that point is, we have to trust Him to make us without breaking us, but such a trust is manifestly impossible where we have usurped His responsibility and invited disaster by choosing our own path. Hence, such a faith in the predestinating thought of God as marked the call of Jeremiah is the very condition that he shall be able to endure through his moral and spiritual tension. Even our Lord Jesus Christ did not arbitrarily choose the supreme tension of His life on earth, for He prayed, like Jeremiah, 'If it be possible, let this cup pass from Me.'

It is, then, the intensity of the inner experience that marks the limits of possible revelation through that experience. Jeremiah was conscious of a glowing fire in his breast, shut up in his bones. It was because he had known that experience that he was able to kindle such a fire of prophetic truth and to become a tester by fire, as in one prophecy he is called:

> 'As a tester have I set thee among My people
>   To know and test their way;
> Rebellious revolters are they all,
>   Walking in slander,
> Bronze and iron are they all,
>   Corrupt are they.
>
> The bellows snort!
>   The lead is consumed by the fire;
> In vain does the smelter smelt,
>   The evil are not plucked out.
> "Rejected silver," men call them,
>   For Yahweh rejects them ' (vi. 27-30).

The fire that tested Judah was the fire of moral and spiritual conviction, the conviction which both commissioned the messenger and supplied his message. Behind the fire there was an invisible hand, feeding the flame, as in Bunyan's vision of the Interpreter's House. What these prophets achieved, they achieved because of that which was achieved in them by the Spirit of God, but by the Spirit of God working most intimately through the moral convictions of the race. These men became the living conscience of their nation, because their own conscience was first alive. That Jeremiah should have shown us this more clearly than the rest, is one of those para-

doxes of religious experience, by which a shy, shrinking,
naturally timid soul will sometimes unveil itself beyond any
other.

But Jeremiah's inner experience, as revealed to us in his
poems, is of importance for another reason. Not only did the
revelation of God come *through* his experience, but in a unique
way, not equalled by any other prophet, the fact of that
experience *itself* became the supreme revelation. He revealed
the meaning of personal religion through the struggles of his
soul against his hard destiny. In him we begin to learn that
a *life* is the fullest revelation of truth—which is one of the
secrets of the Incarnation. As Davidson remarks, with reference to the great prophets who culminate in Jeremiah,
'Prophecy had already taught its truths, its last effort was to
reveal itself in a life' (*H.D.B.*, II, p. 576). Personal religion
indeed means the prophetic consciousness when our prophet
is a Jeremiah. That which was the achievement of the few in
the Old Testament was democratized, through the Person and
Work of our Lord, in the New, that it might become the experience of the many. Jeremiah is fully conscious of what personal
religion means, however surprised he might have been to find
himself taken as the supreme Old Testament type of it. Its
fundamental requirements are enumerated in the prophecy
of the New Covenant:

'Behold, the days come, saith Yahweh, that I will make
a new covenant with the house of Israel, and with the house
of Judah: not according to the covenant that I made with
their fathers in the day that I took them by the hand to
bring them out of the land of Egypt; forasmuch as they
brake My covenant, and I abhorred them, saith Yahweh.
But this is the covenant that I will make with the house of
Israel after those days, said Yahweh: I will put My teaching
in their inward parts, and in their heart will I write it; and
I will be their God, and they shall be My people: and
they shall teach no more every man his neighbour,
and every man his brother, saying, Know Yahweh: for
they shall all know Me, from the least of them unto the
greatest of them, saith Yahweh: for I will forgive their

iniquity, and their sin will I remember no more' (xxxi. 31-34).

We shall have to return at a later point to the Godward aspect of this great prophecy, but it is germane to our present subject to point out that this is a description of personal religion in its individualized experience, and that it implies fundamentally these three things, (1) the moral inwardness of true religion; (2) its dependence on supernatural agencies; (3) its realization of a direct personal fellowship with God. But what is this but to say that it is the extension to all of that experience which was peculiarly Jeremiah's? The first point, the moral inwardness of true religion was that which separated him both from the optimistic prophets of his time, lacking his deep sense of man's sin and God's judgment, and also from the externalism of current religion, with its dependence on outward forms. The second point, the dependence of personal religion of supernatural agencies, seen in the very statement of the divine initiative, is the pre-supposition of all his ministry, and is the anticipation of the New Testament doctrine of the Holy Spirit as the essential basis of the believer's life. The third point, the realization of a direct personal fellowship with God is the most impressive aspect of his autobiography. That autobiography, like Augustine's *Confessions*, is a sustained prayer; his changing moods, his trying circumstances, the spiritual cost of obedience, are all of them brought before God. Jeremiah would fully have understood that fine account which is given by Stephen Grellet of his own practice of self-examination :

'in the evening, when, as was my practice, before I made a record of the manner in which the day had been spent, I came silently and solemnly in the Lord's presence, to inspect my heart, how it had been with me during the day, if I found that it had been turned, even for a short time, unprofitably from God, its centre, I could not retire to rest, till I had a sense of the Divine mercy and forgiveness. My enquiry was not so much whether I had retired from the world to wait upon God, as whether I had retired from God's presence to harbour worldly thoughts' (*Memoirs*, I, p. 42, ed. 1860).

We must frankly recognize the faults and limitations of the prophet, and in particular the bitterness of his maledictions upon his enemies. From the highest Christian standpoint, that admits of no defence. Yet we must remember, in explanation of it, the fact pointed out by Skinner, 'that the whole cause of Yahwe (*sic*) in the world hung on his individual life—upon his inward fidelity to the truth revealed to him, and also on his outward vindication in the sight of men. . . . Either they must go under or he; either they or he must be put to everlasting shame and confusion' (pp. 223, 224). Nor must we forget the point urged in this connection by Sir George Adam Smith, that Jeremiah had no hope of a life beyond death, and that the cause of God must be vindicated here and now, if at all (pp. 334, 340).

But the splendid fact remains that in this prophet we see the human spirit exercising its 'highest dower', in the transformation of life's circumstances into life's eternal meaning. Those lines of Wordsworth's 'Happy Warrior' are an admirable account of Jeremiah's inner life. Unlike the 'Happy Warrior' in so much else, he was like him in being one:

'Who, doomed to go in company with Pain,
And Fear, and Bloodshed, miserable train!
Turns his necessity to glorious gain;
In face of these doth exercise a power
Which is our human nature's highest dower;
Controls them and subdues, transmutes, bereaves
Of their bad influence, and their good receives.'

When we consider his life, within and without, in the light of this truth, and are prepared with Keats to regard this world as 'a vale of soul-making', we can learn from Jeremiah that precious truth of personal religion, that God's chief concern with us is to make a man rather than appoint the most likely applicant to a given job. That truth is needed by every man when he finds himself, like the prophet, committed to an uncongenial or apparently impossible task. To God, the man is always more than the man's success or failure; man is an end in himself, and never the mere means to an end. As to Jesus, the widow and her mites were more than the goodly stones of the temple,[2] so to the God and Father of our Lord Jesus Christ, Jeremiah was more than the walls of Jerusalem.

[2] Cf. Mark xii. 41-44 and xiii. 1, 2.

IV

THE CROSS ABOVE

WE have reviewed in succession the Book, the Life, and the Man, and now we turn to the Man's God, that is, to the theology of the Book of Jeremiah. Here there meets us a principle of method which we cannot ignore. Few but professional students of the Bible realize how completely the method of studying it has changed. From being a text-book it has become a source-book. Historical study has made it impossible for any well-informed person to quote at random this or that verse as though it were an *ipse dixit* of God, settling the questions of morality and religion (not to say those of history and science) once and for all. Every statement about God or man made within the Bible is relative to its own time and given historical setting, and can be understood only in that context; whether it has or has not an extended application, not to say a universal authority, is a question not to be arbitrarily assumed, but to be reverently discussed. What Jeremiah tells us about God is not necessarily true for all time; all that we have the right to ask from a source-book is that it shall be sincere, that it shall endeavour faithfully to represent what was once true in some human experience. But this great, and even yet hardly realized, change in regard to the interpretation of the Bible by no means dispenses with its use for theology, nor should it discredit the ultimate authority of Scripture. The difference now is that instead of jumping to conclusions as to the interpretation of a verse by bringing our own conscious or unconscious ideas about religion to settle the issue, and then investing our result with the authority of a word of God, which is what untrained minds are apt to do still, we try to find out what the words meant historically, and then pass behind the words to the history, and within the history to the human experience it enshrines. But we cannot stop there. We still need to know the universal and authoritative truth about God and man, just as much as people did when they used the Bible as a text-book. Only our method is less superficial, and probably, therefore, less erroneous. We start definitely and avowedly with a human experience, for that is all that any book can give us in the first place. We bring to it a faith that man is somehow made in the image of God, that there is a kinship between human and divine spirits, so that what is true of the less will also be in some sense true of the greater. Without this faith, we can never dare to say anything about God, for we have no means of knowing anything about Him if He is not in some way like ourselves. But with this faith, we turn to the data given us by the Bible, the data of the history of a long and growing fellowship of man and God. Among these data we discern continuous and developing principles which carry conviction, not because they are within the covers of the Bible, but because of what they are, their intrinsic worth. (Such a conviction is really what is meant by a 'value-judgment'.) No doubt we provisionally accept much else, because of the company it keeps, and that is sound enough. But in the last resort our theology is built up on 'value-judgments', whatever intermediate authorities we may recognize. It may well be that with this frank use of a new method we shall not only gain a clearer and truer theology, strong by what it is, rather than by what somebody has said about it, but we shall find some things that were lost, such as the old argument from prophecy, coming back to us in new and better ways.

Jeremiah is an excellent example to illustrate the method, because as Cornill truly says of him, he is 'the psychologist amongst the prophets', and gives us our material more directly in the form in which we want it, as human experience. His theology, i.e. (in the strict and narrower sense) his doctrine of God, is not original in content, for he can hardly be said to have revealed anything about God comparable with the idea of Amos concerning His righteousness, or that of Hosea concerning His love, or that of Isaiah concerning His holiness. The mind of the prophet reached no majestic visions of God, such as those of Isaiah and Ezekiel; it was not gifted with such powers. But there is an originality of use as well as of content; we may take another man's lamp and seek out our own path with it. Jeremiah worked with the ideas of his predecessors, but he made them his own in the best sense by putting them to new uses. In particular his experience of an intimate and familiar fellowship with God threw new light on God's ways and man's. He looked into his own heart in the light of that fellowship, and discovered what the sin he saw about him really meant, and what were its essential roots. He looked up to God as the giver of the best in his own experience, the God who promised that if he uttered the best he knew, he should be as God's mouth, and by this very experience of himself learnt more about God's ways. Jeremiah stood on other men's shoulders, but standing there, he used his opportunity to reach higher than all of them.

In an interesting poem, Jeremiah tells us the impression made on him by the life of the city when he brought his village eyes to bear upon it:

'Run ye about in the streets of Jerusalem,
    See ye and know,
And seek in her broad places,
    Whether ye find a man—
If there is one doing justice,
    Seeking the truth—
        Then will I pardon her.
For when they say, "As Yahweh lives,"
    They swear to a lie. . . .

Thou hast smitten them, but they were not sore,
    Consumed them, they took not correction;
They hardened their faces beyond rock,
    They refused to return.

I said, "These are only the poor,
    They are foolish;
For they know not the way of Yahweh,
    The rule of their God.

" I will get me to the great men,
 With them I will speak;
For *they* know the way of Yahweh,
 The rule of their God."
But *they* have all broken the yoke,
 And snapped the thongs' (v. 1-5).

But this fact of man's universal failure to be what God would have him to be is a fact of observation not traced to any dogma of original sin. On the contrary, it is an enigma, beyond explanation; why is it, the prophet asks (viii. 5 f.), that 'every one turneth to his course, as a horse that rusheth headlong in the battle'? For there is surely some instinct in man that should urge him to obedience:

‘Even the stork in the heavens knows her seasons
 And dove and swift and swallow keep the time of their
  coming,
 But as for my people, they know not the rule of Yahweh'
  (viii. 7).

A convict, who has recently given us his impressions of English prison life,[1] tells us that he had to make Gilbert White's *Natural History of Selborne* last him for a month, and that this concentrated interest in the book was enhanced by the swifts that came in May and built under the eaves opposite his cell, 'the descendants of the birds Gilbert White had studied and recorded 150 years ago.' They brought to him their message of the free country, but they did not suggest to him what they did to the prophet, the contrast between their obedience and man's disobedience to the divine order, their true nature. At the parting of ways, Israel refused to stand and ask for the ancient road to prosperity (vi. 16). How strange and unnatural this forgetfulness of God on the part of the nation seems to the prophet:

‘Forgets a maiden her ornaments,
 A bride her girdle?
Yet My people have forgotten Me,
 Days without number' (ii. 32).

[1] *Among the Broad-Arrow Men*, by ‘B. 2.15', p. 46.

M

Skinner points out (p. 148) that the particular sins most
severely condemned by the prophet are untruthfulness and
sexual profligacy, both of them sins affecting the personal
relations of men in society to a marked degree. It is clear
that the prophet is constrained to carry his analysis of sin, not
only beyond the nation to the individual, but from the external
acts of the individual to the heart from which evil springs.
He had learnt from personal experience:

> 'Deeper is the heart than all else,
> And sick is it; who can know it?' (xvii. 9).

This recognition of the *inwardness* of sin is one of the definite
contributions of Jeremiah to the truth about man. It is in
'the stubbornness of the heart' that the evil begins (vii. 24,
v. 23, ix. 14, xxiii. 17). We must remember that the heart,
in Hebrew psychology, is *not* primarily the seat of the
emotions, as with us, but of the intellectual and especially the
volitional side of life, so that the best translation of the Hebrew
terms ' heart ', as here, would be the 'will'. Because Jeremiah has thus penetrated to one of the cardinal facts of
morality and religion, he is able so clearly and emphatically
to assert the futility of external worship, as in the 'Temple
Sermon'. There must be the inner consecration of the will,
which is expressed by the figure of circumcision (iv. 4). The
ear itself must be consecrated, if there is to be responsive hearing (vi. 10)—another point drawn from Hebrew psychology,
since the peripheral organs are conceived to have a psychical
and ethical quality and function of their own.[2] But the very
need for this radical change throws the prophet back on God.
He only can work that miracle on which the prophet's hope
of a future for Israel depends, as is seen in the declaration of
the New Covenant. For there is a certain momentum in moral
evil, which carries on the will through what we should call
the law of habit to a definite hardening, which is part of the
penalty. The very phrase ' stubbornness of the will ' denotes
its firmness or fixity in evil purpose. That penalty is most
forcibly expressed:

[2] See *The Christian Doctrine of Man*, by H. Wheeler Robinson, pp. 23 ff.

> ' Can the African change his skin,
> And the leopard his marks?
> Then ye, also, are able to do good,
> Trained to do evil! ' (xiii. 23).

By long refusal to receive discipline, 'faithfulness has perished and is cut off from their mouth' (vii. 28). So there comes at last a certain wilful abandonment of self-control, crying 'Desperate! for we will walk after our own devices, and we will do every one after the fixity of his evil will' (xviii. 12, cf. ii. 25).

This, then, was the first result to which the prophet's own fellowship with God had led him, that sin is not primarily the deed of a nation disloyal to its national God, but springs from the inner attitude, the wills of the individuals who make the nation, and that the result of long continuance in the evil will is a hardening of the purpose, and indifference to the consequences, from which there is practically no hope of recovery in man himself. In full accordance with this result, indeed, as its complementary truth, he conceives Yahweh in a new way, as the trier of heart and kidneys, that is, of the will and the emotions. For the first time in Hebrew religion we reach the declaration of this truth, familiar to the thought of the Christian, and, indeed, familiar to the religion of post-exilic Judaism, as in the closing words of the 139th psalm which teaches the omniscience and omnipresence of God:

> 'Search me, O God, and know my will:
> Try me and know my thoughts:
> And see if there be any way of wickedness in me,
> And lead me in the way everlasting'
>   (Ps. cxxxix. 23, 24).

The pioneer of that cardinal truth for personal religion is Jeremiah, and he won his way to it by a deep personal experience of God, for he brings together his confession of the heart's evil and his conviction of God's inner testing:

> 'Deeper is the heart than all else
> And sick is it: who can know it?

I am Yahweh, searching the heart
Testing the feelings (*lit.*, kidneys);
To give to a man as his ways,
As the fruit of his deeds' (xvii. 9, 10).

More than once does Jeremiah return to that thought of
God, so characteristic of him. In his cry for vengeance on
his plotting enemies, he appeals to One who can make no
mistake, because He knows man from within:

'Yahweh of Hosts, judging righteously,
Testing feelings and will (*lit.*, kidneys and heart)
Let me see Thy vengeance on them
For to Thee have I bared my cause' (xi. 20; cf. xx. 12).

Yahweh, who had made His prophet the tester or trier of
Israel (vi. 27), was Himself the supreme Tester of their inner
life:
'A God Who is near am I
And not a God who is far;
Shall a man hide in secret
And I not see him?
Is it not heaven and earth I fill?
—Oracle of Yahweh'
(xxiii. 23, 24, with the Versions).

The true glory of life, says Jeremiah, is not knowledge,
strength or wealth, but fellowship with Yahweh, whose deeds
are characterized by covenant-grace, justice, and righteousness (xi. 23, 24). In an impressive figure, which has inspired
part of the first psalm, the prophet compares the man who
enjoys this fellowship and trusts in such a God with 'a tree
planted by the waters, and that spreadeth out his roots by the
river, and shall not fear when heat cometh, but his leaf shall
be green; and shall not be careful in the year of drought,
neither shall cease from yielding fruit,' whilst the opposite
type of man, whose will is not one with God's, whose confidence is in human strength alone, is like some stunted shrub
of 'the parched places in the wilderness, a salt land and not

inhabited' (xvii. 5-8). That is a nobler and wider conception
of personal religion than we find in the first Psalm, which
defines it within the limits of Jewish legalism, the observance
of the Law; the nobility and breadth of Jeremiah's words is
characteristic of the prophetic religion at its highest. The
figure of growth may suggest a certain inevitability in the
working out of life, for good or for evil, given such and such
conditions. The reward of fellowship with God and the
penalty of self-will and isolation from Him are not arbitrary,
but follow in what we should call a natural sequence, though
for the prophet 'nature' is God's. So when he would confirm the prophecy of the New Covenant, he compares its cer-
tainty with that of the rule of nature by Yahweh, 'who giveth
the sun for a light by day, and the ordinances of the moon and
the stars for a light by night, which stirreth up the sea, that
the waves thereof roar' (xxxi. 35). So also it is with the wrath
of God against sin, of which the prophet speaks so often and
so sternly. 'How else should I do, because of the daughter
of my people?' cries Yahweh; 'shall I not visit them for these
things, shall not My soul be avenged on such a nation as this?'
(ix. 7, 9).

All things that come to man are conceived as coming by
the direct personal action of God, and the Bible knows nothing
of 'natural law' in our modern sense, as something working
in independence of personal action. Hence, the very consequences of sin are stated as the direct activity of God, as in
the command to the prophet, 'Take the cup of the wine of
this fury at My hand, and cause all the nations, to whom I
shall send thee, to drink it. And they shall drink and reel to
and fro, and be mad, because of the sword that I will send
among them' (xxv. 15, 16). The sword is here the advance of
the Babylonians, as the instrument of God's wrath, and the
whole experience is conceived as a cup to be drunk, pro-
ducing intoxication.

But there are elements in Jeremiah's idea of God deeper than
the simple reaction of righteous wrath against rebellion. Just
as his experience of fellowship with God taught him more of
the essential meaning of sin, so it taught him more of the
divine nature, and of what sin means in relation to that nature.

We may compare the similar, though less developed, theology
of Hosea, between whom and Jeremiah there are so many
links of spiritual kinship.   Hosea also traced the evil of his
times beyond the visible deed to an inner spirit; 'the spirit
of whoredom hath caused them to err' (iv. 12); 'their doings
will not suffer them to turn unto their God; for the spirit of
whoredom is within them, and they know not Yahweh' (v. 4).
Hosea also is deeply impressed by the wrong that this disloyalty does to the grace of Yahweh, the forsaken husband of
His people.   Now, directly we reach that conception of sin
we see it in a new light.   It is no longer simple disobedience
to a command, the act of a slave; it is the churlish ingratitude
of an unresponsive child, blind to all the father's care and
love.   Sin, man's characteristic act and attitude, and grace,
which is God's, are always so inter-related.   As we learn more
of the one, so we do of the other, and the fellowship of God
and man progressively reveals both sides.   Just as man's sin
is seen to have a darker meaning than simple disobedience, so
God's grace finds new opportunities of revealing its hidden
wealth of patience and self-sacrifice through the very challenge
of man's sin.   Something of that is already involved in the title
which Jeremiah gives to Yahweh, *Chasidh* (iii. 12), or the
'Loyal-in-love', as Sir George Adam Smith well renders it.   It
attributes to Him the quality of covenant-love, the sense of
duty within love, such as the thirteenth chapter of 1 Corin-
thians makes explicit.   It is thus the reproach of hurt affection,
faithlessness to the faithful one, that finds utterance in Jeremiah's earliest oracles, as he confronts the nation:

> 'I remember the troth of thy youth,
>   Thy love as a bride,
> Thy following Me through the desert,
>   The land unsown. . . .
> What wrong found your fathers in Me,
>   That so far they broke from Me? . . .
> Nor said they:
>   Where is the Lord who carried us up
>   From the land of Egypt,
>   Who led us through the desert,

Land of waste and chasms,
Land of drought and barren,
A land which nobody crosses,
Nor mankind settles upon it.
And I brought you into a garden,
   To feed on its fruit and its wealth. . . .
Twain the wrongs My people have wrought—
   Me have they left.
The Fount of live water,
To hew themselves cisterns,
Cisterns broken,
That cannot hold water! ' (ii. 1-13,
                from Sir George Adam Smith's version.)

There is an appeal to this very relation of Yahweh to his people, as called forth by the miseries of a drought:

'Thou Hope of Israel, Yahweh!
   Its Saviour in times of distress,
Why art Thou like a stranger in the land,
   Like a traveller staying for a night?

Why art Thou like a man asleep,
   Like a strong man unable to save?
For Thou art amongst us, O Yahweh!
   We are called by Thy name; do not leave us' (xvi. 8, 9).

Because of this covenant-love, Yahweh cannot punish without pain to Himself, a pain which finds expression even as He delivers sentence:

'I have forsaken My house,
   I have abandoned My heritage,
I have given My heart's beloved
   Into the grasp of her foes.
My heritage has become to Me
   Like a lion in the forest;
She has uttered against Me her voice,
   Therefore I hate her.

Is My heritage to Me a gay wild-bird,
With wild-birds round and against her?
Go gather all beasts of the field,
    Bring them hither to eat.
Many shepherds have ruined My vineyard,
    Have trampled My portion;
They have turned My delightful portion
    Into a desolate wilderness.
They have made it a waste; it mourns;
    On Me (lies) the waste!
Wasted is all the land,
    No man pays heed! ' (xii. 7-11).

So again, in xxxi. 20:

'Is Ephraim My dearest son,
    My darling child?
That as oft as I speak against him
    I needs must remember him still?
Therefore My heart yearns for him,
    I *must* have mercy upon him.'

But the sense of what the sin of Israel must cost Israel's God finds most striking expression in the short personal oracle to Baruch, which seems to close Baruch's biography of the prophet (xlv.):

'Thou hast said, Alas now for me!
    For Yahweh has added sorrow to my pain;
I am weary with my groaning,
    And rest I have not found.

Thus shalt thou say unto him,
    Thus hath said Yahweh,
Lo, that which I have built,
    Am *I* pulling down,
And that which I have planted,
    Am *I* plucking up;
And *thou*, seek'st thou for thyself great things? '

In this striking oracle we see comfort brought to the sorrow of man by the realization of the sorrow of God. Baruch is overwhelmed by the sense of the failure of the prophet's work and of his own, and the prophet recalls him to the thought of God's failure. Is there room for his own complaint, in presence of the tragedy of God's defeated purpose for Israel, and all this means to God? For God must pull down the building of many generations, raised by his own hands, uproot the tree He has planted and nurtured, for righteousness' sake. There is hardly a passage in the Old Testment which gives us a more impressive glimpse of the eternal cross in the heart of God, the bitterness of His disappointment with man.

Yet bitterness is not the right word. Behind that disappointment there is the infinite patience of God, the power to accomplish His purpose in other ways, if not in this. There is something of this thought underlying the parable of the potter, whom the prophet saw working at his wheel. If the vessel was not to the mind of the potter he crushed the clay together and reshaped it (xviii. 1 f.). How will Yahweh accomplish the purpose of His defeated love for His people?

The principle of the answer to this question has already been given in the quotation of the familiar prophecy of the New Covenant (xxxi. 31-34). Because the root of all the trouble is in the evil will of individual men, and habit has made it impossible for them of themselves to repent, the prophet dares to conceive some new realization of the eternal covenant-relation of Yahweh and Israel. Yahweh will not again give an external law, which men will disobey as before; He will work from within and by a spiritual change inspire a new and effective knowledge of Himself in the hearts of men. The new relation will be upheld like that between the prophet and his God in the intimacies of personal religion, which has got beyond the stage at which a human teacher is needed. The old sins will be forgiven, and the new knowledge of God shall make impossible new sins such as the old. We must remember what a prophet means by the knowledge of God—no intellectual system of belief, but a personal fellowship with Him. *How* that new relation is to be established Jeremiah cannot say; he would have thought it unnecessary to speculate, for is it not bound to be the act of God, and therefore beyond man's comprehension? Ezekiel, who also saw the need for divine activity, conceived it more materialistically as a resurrection of the nation from the valley of dry bones, by the creative work of God, and by the life-giving power of His Spirit replacing the breath of men, whilst that new life is to be maintained by a new and elaborated ritual. But Jeremiah, psychologist as he is, is content to emphasize the inner conditions of such divine activity, the individual relation, the inner change, the touch of God, leaving the external media of the change to Him. In this way Yahweh will reconstitute the destroyed society of His people from transformed individuals.

We are, however, able to say in which direction the prophet looked for what may be called the raw material of this divine activity. He saw, and later experience was only a confirmation of his insight (which was shared by Ezekiel), that the future of the nation lay with the exiles in Babylon, not with those who remained. He bluntly compared the two halves of the people after 597, viz., its better deported class, and its worse remaining elements, with two baskets of figs, one good and one bad (xxiv.). He sent an oracle to these exiles in Babylon, exhorting them to accept the conditions of their lot as God's will, and to identify their immediate future with that of their captors:

'Build ye houses and dwell in them, and plant gardens and eat the fruit of them; take ye wives, and beget sons and daughters; and take wives for your sons, and give your daughters to husbands, that they may bear sons and daughters; and multiply ye there, and be not diminished. And seek the peace of the city whither I have caused you to be carried away captive, and pray unto Yahweh for it: for in the peace therefore, shall ye have peace' (xxix. 5-7).

In other words, he tells them Babylon will be their home for two or three generations, which is exactly the meaning of the round number of seventy years (10). Then, in the fulness of the time, they shall seek Yahweh and find Him, seeking Him with all their heart (13), and He will change their fortunes and gather them home. There could be no lovelier picture to leave us than that in which the prophet imagines the future realization of the covenant-bond:

> 'The people finds grace in the desert,
> Escaped from the sword;
> When Israel goes to his rest,
> From afar doth Yahweh appear:—
> "With a love everlasting I love thee,
> Therefore with kindness I draw thee."

> Once more I will build thee securely,
> O virgin of Israel!
> Once more thou shalt deck thee with timbrels,
> Go forth in the dance of the merry;
> Once more thou shalt plant with (thy) vineyards
> Samaria's hills!' (xxxi. 2-5.)

In that vision there is something of the Parable of the Prodigal Son, better called that of the Forgiving Father. It needs but for the penitent Israel to say, 'I will arise and go to my Father,' and straightway Yahweh Himself comes forth to meet His son, to embrace him and say, 'With a love from of old I love thee; therefore in kindness I draw thee.' Such is the final victory of grace, suffering because it loves, and winning because it suffers. So journeys end in lovers' meeting.

As we look back over the road we have travelled, we can see how great was the contribution made by Jeremiah to religion. The subsequent books of the Bible are in themselves a sufficient proof; without Jeremiah they would be far other than they are. Though his younger contemporary, Ezekiel, does not name him, this prophet shows the influence of Jeremiah in many parallels of thought and expression. As it was given to Ezekiel to exercise a most potent influence on the outer forms of post-exilic religion, so was it the privilege of Jeremiah to inspire its inner pieties, as no other did. We may see this in particular in the Psalter, and at its finest in the climax of the seventy-third Psalm, with its confident surrender of the soul to God in a fellowship that desires no other,

and fears no foe, not even death. Every attentive and thoughtful reader of the Psalms will be constrained to admit the truth
of Sir George Adam Smith's eloquent words, 'the personal
piety which henceforth flourished in Israel as it had never
flourished before, weaving its delicate tendrils about the ruins
of the state, the city and the altar, and (as the Psalms show)
blooming behind the shelter of the Law like a garden of lilies
within a fence of thorns, sprang from seeds in Jeremiah's own
heart, and was watered by his tears, and the sweat of his
spiritual agonies' (pp. 373, 374). The reverence felt for him
in later generations as the prophet of the fall of the holy city
and of David's throne, the prophet whose words were so
amply vindicated, is seen in the legends that grew up around
his name, as the divinely appointed keeper of tabernacle and
ark and altar of incense until the future gathering of the people
(2 Macc. ii. 1 ff.), or in that fine story of Judas Maccabæus
dreaming a dream on the eve of his victory over Nicanor, in
which he saw Jeremiah appear:

> ' " of venerable age and exceeding glory, and wonderful and
> most majestic was the dignity around him," whilst an
> interpreting voice said of him, " this is the lover of the
> brethren, he who prayeth much for the people and the holy
> city, Jeremiah the prophet of God : and Jeremiah stretching
> forth his right hand delivered to Judas a sword of gold, and
> in giving it addressed him thus, Take the holy sword, a gift
> from God, wherewith thou shalt smite down the adver-
> saries "' (*ib*. xv. 13-16).

In the New Testament there are between forty and fifty
quotations or echoes of the Book of Jeremiah, but we chiefly
remember the fact that some men could find no better interpretation of Jesus than to see in him Jeremiah come back to
his people.

Another notable stream of influence emanating from Jeremiah flows into the idea of the suffering Servant of Yahweh,
as conceived in Deutero-Isaiah. If we had to find a definite
historical model for that exilic picture, none would be more
fitting than Jeremiah, and even though we regard it as a

portrait of Israel personified, as I think we must, yet the life
and sufferings of Jeremiah may well have influenced the por-
traiture. Indeed, there is direct proof of this. Not only does
such a phrase as 'I was not rebellious, neither turned away
back' (Is. l. 5) seem to be drawn from the obedience of Jeremiah to the divine compulsion within (Jer. xx. 9), but the
comparison of the Servant with 'a lamb that is led to the
slaughter' (Is. liii. 7) is verbally borrowed from Jeremiah's own
description of himself, when surrounded by plotting enemies:
'I was like a gentle lamb that is led to the slaughter' (Jer.
xi. 19). We have but to think of the course of Jeremiah's life,
the physical and spiritual suffering endured through the sin
of his people, his isolation from them, yet his identification
with them, so that it was his free choice that kept him with
Gedaliah after the fall of the city—we have but to think of all
this to see how aptly the Servant of Yahweh epitomizes the
prophet's life. Through the Servant, and more directly still,
Jeremiah became an influence of the great moment in the life
of our Lord, whom the New Testament calls by Jeremiah's
figure, 'The Lamb of God.' It was Jesus who first united the
figure of the Suffering Servant with the traditional figure of
the Messiah, and in so doing gave a new content of meaning
to the old name. It was Jesus who lifted the sacrificial suffering which Jeremiah experienced in history, and Deutero-Isaiah
interpreted in idea, to a new level of meaning and a new purity
of expression. Is it not significant that our Lord should have
taken the prophecy of the New Covenant into the Holy of
Holies of the Upper Room, and offered His own work as its
fulfilment?

Along yet another line we may see the influence of the
prophet. Such suffering as his, so continuous and so undeserved, was bound to raise the problem of the suffering of
the innocent, which was the chief anxiety of the more
reflective minds of Israel. Jeremiah himself had felt it (xii.),
and it reappears in the Book of his contemporary Habakkuk,
as well as in certain psalms. But it was to be treated centuries
afterwards on the grand scale in the Book of Job. Now the
poetry of the Book of Job, the poet's expansion of the old
tradition, begins with an elaborate curse of life, closely

modelled on Jeremiah's utterances. The imitation is obvious, and the intention seems to be (as Duhm has suggested) to use Jeremiah's indictment of life as the basis of that which the later poet wished to draw, since ' the most anxious reader could take no objection to that which so great a prophet had done before the poet's hero'. In the Book of Job the nearest approach to a solution of the problem of innocent suffering is to say that it may serve the hidden purpose of God by eliciting the witness of a life to the reality of disinterested religion. Plato said that the reality of disinterested justice could be demonstrated only by taking away all that might seem to make it worth while. The Book of Job uses an experience of suffering comparable with that of Jeremiah as a proof of the reality of disinterested religion. Such a life, then, has a value all its own, when its seems valueless; it is worth while to God, even when it ceases to seem worth anything to the man himself. The writer of the Book of Job would have agreed with Bourget's most suggestive phrase, ' nothing is lost when we make an offering of it.'[3]

When we bring together these three lines of indubitable influence exercised by the life of Jeremiah, and note how the realities of that life become more explicit in idea through that which it inspires in others, we seem able to make some kind of synthesis of all three of them. The contribution of personal religion (Psalms) is made through a life of sacrificial suffering (The Servant of Yahweh), which has an intrinsic value to God (Job). Is not that synthesis in itself a true line of approach to the understanding of a greater Cross than Jeremiah's? Just as we may best draw near to the holy mystery of the Lord's Person by thinking of the prophetic consciousness raised to the level of the filial, as it was in Christ, so we may think of the offering of the Cross of Calvary as the offering of personal religion, realized in sacrifice, and having in itself—not in any penalty artificially inflicted on it—but in itself, in what it is, a positive value to God.

' It is the Kingdom, not the Christ, that the prophets primarily proclaim; but, as the facts of Israel's history make clear the divine method of working through great personali-

[3] See ' The Cross of Job ', p. 19 passim.

ties for the benefit of the community, the great personalities whom God raises up to act and suffer for His people become the prophecy of the great Actor, the great Sufferer, whom God must yet raise up.[4] The truth of these words may be seen when we reflect on the fellowship with God in the suffering which sin must always bring to holiness. When we ask how sin is possible at all in a world where the holy God is ultimately all in all, we can answer only by speaking of some kind of self-limitation on the part of God. In Him even the sinner lives and moves and has his being; yet the sinner's sin must lie beyond the circle of God's holiness. How does God deal with that fact of sin when He forgives the penitent sinner? Some have said, and still say, that He thereafter ignores it, so that the Atonement is simply the effective revelation of the forgiving love of God. Attractive as the apparent simplicity of that view may seem, it does not do justice to the nature of sin or to the mystery of the Cross of Christ. It does not do justice to the experience of the human saint when brought into relation with the sin of men. In a real sense he must suffer through sin, and the nobler his saintliness, the deeper his suffering. Apart from all the physical and mental sufferings of the prophet Jeremiah because of his mission, the very contact with the sin of Israel must have been something of a crucifixion. How much deeper the suffering of Jesus in presence of the world's sin! But is not that depth of suffering the earthly realization of the heavenly law, that sin taken up into holiness *must* be transformed into suffering? As God's self-limited circle expands to take in that sin of the world which He cannot ignore, the sin becomes so much suffering for the Holy God—in no other way can it enter the circle of His holiness. James Denney seems drawn towards such a view when he writes: ' I have often wondered whether we might not say that the Christian doctrine of the Atonement just meant that in Christ God took the responsibility of evil upon Himself, and somehow subsumed evil under good.'[5] The peril, as he so clearly saw, is that we may minimize the true nature of sin in order to bring it within the divine circle. But that peril

---

[4] H. L. Goudge, in *Ency. of Religion and Ethics*, x. 748.
[5] *Letters of Principal James Denney to his Family and Friends*, p. 187.

seems to be avoided if, *within God*, the irrationality of sin is transformed into the mystery of the eternal Cross, the Cross within the very heart of God. To be called into the fellowship of God is to be called into the fellowship of that suffering for sin. As we realize what that meant for Jeremiah, we may be brought to realize something of what it meant to the perfect fellowship of Jesus with His Father—a far deeper suffering and a far higher Atonement. We cannot lift the veil that hides *His* inner life from us; we can but reverently look when His own hand lifts it for a moment in the temptation in the wilderness, in the prayer of Gethsemane, in the cry of the Cross, ' My God, My God, why hast Thou forsaken Me? '[6] But the fact that Jeremiah has so opened his heart to us, and has shown us so fully the cost of such spiritual achievement as was his, may teach us something of the mystery of the greater cost of the offering of the Son of God, the temporal realization of the eternal Cross of God Himself.

[6] Cf. W. Temple, *The Nature of Personality*, p. xxxi.: ' We who are Christians remember that the Godhead never shone forth in Christ so effulgently as in the moment when He felt Himself forsaken of God.'